THE

5 IN 10

DESSERT COOKBOOK

---

5 Ingredients in
10 Minutes or Less

NATALIE HAUGHTON

A JOHN BOSWELL ASSOCIATES / KING HILL PRODUCTIONS BOOK

HEARST BOOKS

NEW YORK

Library of Congress Cataloging-in-Publication Data

Haughton, Natalie.
    The 5 in 10 dessert cookbook : 5 ingredients in 10 minutes or less / Natalie Haughton.
      p.   cm.
    "A John Boswell Associates/King Hill Productions book."
    Includes index.
    ISBN 0-688-04561-8
    1. Desserts. 2. Quick and easy cookery. I. Title. II. Title.
    Five in ten dessert cookbook.
    TX773.H334   1993
    641.8′6—dc20
                                             93-14271
                                              CIP

Printed in the United States of America

First Edition

1 2 3 4 5 6 7 8 9 10

Book design by Barbara Cohen Aronica

CONTENTS

Whatever the occasion, here's a dessert to match it: sophisticated and international Tiramisu, especially rich like Mile-High Mud Pie and Lemon Raspberry Trifle or just lots of fun like Pineapple Jelly-Roll Swirl.

No one will believe your Boston Cream Pie, Italian Cassata, Kahlúa Pie and Almond Peach Tart are *5 in 10* desserts.

Southern-Style Banana Pudding, Chocolate Raisin Bread Pudding, Raspberry Mousse and Strawberry Pineapple Cloud are a few of the spooned-up sweets offered here.

4. ESPECIALLY CHOCOLATE 61

Quick tricks with this favorite dark flavor include 10-Minute Brownies, Chocolate Pots de Crème, Chocolate Truffle Torte and Chocolate Orange Fondue.

5. WARM DESSERTS 82

From the oven and the microwave, these sweets range from Bananas in Rum Cream Sauce and Pineapple Fritters to Apple Crisp and Microwave Peach Cobbler with Buttermilk Biscuit Topping.

6. COOL FRUITS 102

Variety and color abound in fast, refreshing desserts, such as Citrus Cherry Wine Compote, Tropical Fruit Salad with Toasted Coconut, Pears Poached in Red Wine with sweet spices and Pineapple Melba Dessert.

INTRODUCTION

Homemade desserts never go out of style. But as our time and energy resources become scarcer, they are often given up as just too much extra work. How many times have you spotted a tempting, luscious-sounding dessert, only to be turned off by the long list of ingredients or the time—you don't have—required to bake even a simple cake. Oh, I'll just pick up a pint of ice cream or a store-bought pie, you think, even though dessert, eaten last, polishes the perception of the entire meal.

That's where *The 5 in 10 Dessert Cookbook* comes to the rescue. It offers over 165 sweet creations that look and taste great and get you in and out of the kitchen in a hurry. That's because each recipe calls for only five ingredients or fewer and has a cooking time of ten minutes or less. Some are eaten immediately, while others require a bit of unattended time in the refrigerator or freezer to set up or chill.

To accomplish this feat, prodigious use is made of top-quality components: refrigerated pie crusts, already peeled and sliced frozen peaches, loaf cakes, angel food cakes, premium ice creams and the like. Creative assembly combined with homemade custards, fillings and toppings add up to showstopper desserts in no time. Fresh fruits, which are nutritious as well as delicious, and good both hot and cold, are a favorite item. Apple, berries and pears are caramelized, pureed, sautéed, poached in wine, drizzled with chocolate sauce, whipped into mousses, baked and broiled.

Because so few ingredients are used in each dessert, it is especially important that they be top quality. Go out of your way to purchase a good brand of cake, the ripest fruit and premium ice cream. If you find you make dessert often, it makes sense to stock up on a certain number of staples and convenience products for a *5 in 10* dessert pantry. With these items squirreled away, you can whip up any number of fabulous desserts on a moment's notice.

Consider your cupboard: chocolate chips, sweetened cocoa powder, walnuts and pecans, graham crackers, chocolate and vanilla wafer cookies, sugar, pure vanilla extract, pudding and pie filling mixes, ready-to-serve cookie and graham cracker crumb crusts, dried fruits, seedless raspberry jam. For the refrigerator: cream cheese, heavy cream, milk, eggs, a package of prepared pie crust, sweetened whipped cream in a pressurized container. In the freezer, stow away a ready-made pie crust—either flaky pastry or cookie crumb—bags of quick-frozen unsweetened peaches and raspberries, ice cream, a pint of sorbet, perhaps a frozen all-butter pound cake or chocolate loaf cake. Choose seasonal fruits with an eye to color and flavor. With these few supplies on hand, you'll be ready for dessert whenever dessert calls you.

When you're preparing dessert in such a hurry, be prepared to be flexible. When it's necessary, substitute what you have on hand. For example, a pie made in a plain pie crust might work just as well in a graham cracker or cookie crumb crust and vice versa. Strawberries and raspberries can often be interchanged, as can apples and pears, peaches and nectarines, dried apricots and raisins or prunes.

Much is made, too, of modern equipment to save every second possible. Quick skillet desserts, such as sautéed Bananas in Rum

Cream Sauce, microwaved 10-Minute Brownies, flash-baked cookies, food-processor Chocolate Mousse and speedy stove-top stirred custards and old-fashioned puddings add up to a surprisingly large repertoire any cook will be proud of.

Included are a wide variety of cakes, pies and tarts, creations especially striking for entertaining, a whole chapter of dark, rich chocolate sweets, puddings, mousses, hot and cold fruits, ice creams and other frozen desserts, cookies, candies and even sweet drinks. These fast, appealing recipes are designed for both novice and seasoned cooks alike, whether it's something like Southern-Style Banana Pudding for a weekday after-supper sweet or a Chocolate Truffle Torte for the grand finale to a weekend dinner party.

1 DESIGNED FOR ENTERTAINING

It's always fun to dazzle guests with stylish showstopper desserts. For *5 in 10* cooks, that means serving simple yet spectacular-tasting creations, some with unusual presentations, others with international flair. Apple Galette, a paper-thin, free-form tart, Tiramisu, Broiled Strawberries Brûlée, Apricot Charlotte and Lemon Raspberry Trifle are just a few of the desserts that can be made in a jiffy.

For more novel, conversation-piece desserts that will be the talk of the party, whip up a Double Strawberry Pie, Mile-High Mud Pie or Strawberry Chocolate Truffle Pizza. Or add a touch of drama with a flambéed classic, such as Crepes Suzettes or Cherries Jubilee.

These recipes rely on fresh and dried fruits; specialty cheeses, such as Brie, Gorgonzola, ricotta and mascarpone; prepared pound cakes and cannoli shells; and an assortment of flavorings, fillings and toppings: chocolate, packaged pie glaze, nuts, jarred preserves, store-bought ice creams, sorbets and whipped cream. Don't stint on the quality of the ingredients; purchase the best available.

While some of the desserts require last-minute preparation (they shouldn't be prepared ahead because they won't hold), others in this group will be easier for entertaining if they are made in advance and stored in the refrigerator or freezer until serving time.

APPLE GALETTE

This free-form puff pastry tart looks elegant and tastes great. Serve with vanilla ice cream for a special treat.

1 sheet frozen puff pastry ($\frac{1}{2}$ of a 17$\frac{1}{4}$-ounce package)
3 medium Granny Smith apples
2 tablespoons butter
2 tablespoons sugar
$\frac{1}{2}$ teaspoon ground cinnamon

1. Preheat the oven to 450 degrees F. Thaw the pastry only 15 to 20 minutes; it should still be very cold. Peel, core and cut the apples into $\frac{1}{4}$- to $\frac{3}{8}$-inch-thick slices.

2. With a rolling pin, roll the puff pastry sheet out on an ungreased cookie sheet to an 11$\frac{1}{2}$-inch square. Fold the edges of the pastry up $\frac{1}{2}$ inch on all sides, pressing with your fingers to form a rim; pinch at the corners.

3. Arrange the apple slices in an attractive pattern over the puff pastry square. Place the butter in a small glass bowl. Microwave on High for 20 to 30 seconds, or until melted. Brush over the apples.

4. Mix together the sugar and cinnamon. Sprinkle evenly over the apple slices.

5. Bake for 10 minutes, or until the edges of the puff pastry are light brown. Cool for a few minutes. Cut into 9 pieces and serve.

9 SERVINGS

APRICOT CHARLOTTE

Here is an instant, elegant charlotte made in individual dessert dishes rather than in a single large mold. Garnish the tops with sliced almonds, if you like.

1 can (16 ounces) apricot halves
1 cup heavy cream
2 tablespoons powdered sugar
3 tablespoons Cognac or brandy
8 ladyfingers

1. Drain the apricots well, discarding the syrup. Chop the apricots into small pieces.

2. In a medium bowl with an electric mixer on high speed, beat the cream and powdered sugar until stiff peaks form. Stir in the chopped apricots and 1 tablespoon of the Cognac, mixing until well blended.

3. Split the ladyfingers in half. Drizzle the remaining 2 tablespoons Cognac over the cut sides of the ladyfingers.

4. Place 2 ladyfinger halves, cut-sides up, in each of 4 dessert dishes or stemmed goblets. Spoon half of the apricot cream over the ladyfingers. Cover with 2 more ladyfinger halves, cut-sides up. Top with the remaining apricot cream. Serve immediately or cover and refrigerate until serving time.

4 SERVINGS

BANANA PUFF PASTRY TART

Plan to serve this warm out of the oven. It's yummy!

1 sheet frozen puff pastry (1/2 of a 17 1/4-ounce package)
3 bananas
3 tablespoons butter
3 tablespoons light brown sugar
1/2 teaspoon ground cinnamon

1. Preheat the oven to 450 degrees F. Thaw the pastry sheet only 15 to 20 minutes; it should still be very cold. Peel and slice the bananas and place them in a medium bowl. Place the butter in a small glass bowl. Microwave on High for 20 to 30 seconds, or until melted. Add the melted butter, brown sugar and cinnamon to the bananas. Toss gently to mix well.

2. With a rolling pin, roll the puff pastry sheet out on an ungreased cookie sheet to a 10 1/2- or 11-inch square. With a knife, cut and round off the 4 corners to make a circle shape.

3. Fold the edges of the pastry up 1/2 inch all the way around the circle, pressing and pinching with your fingers to form a rim. Arrange the banana slices in an attractive pattern over the puff pastry circle.

4. Bake for 10 minutes, or until the edges of the puff pastry are light brown. Cool for a few minutes. With a sharp knife, cut into wedges. Serve immediately.

6 TO 8 SERVINGS

CHERRIES JUBILEE

For a truly dramatic dessert, have the ice cream ready to top with the flaming sauce. Heat the brandy just until fumes are produced, as it is the fumes that ignite. To avoid any flare-up, do not allow the brandy to boil.

1 can (16 to 17 ounces) dark sweet pitted cherries
1 orange
1 tablespoon cornstarch
1½ pints premium ice cream
¼ cup brandy or kirsch

1. Drain the juice from the cherries into a medium nonreactive saucepan; set the cherries aside. Grate the colored zest and squeeze the juice from the orange; set aside.

2. Stir the cornstarch into the cherry juice until well blended. Heat to boiling over medium heat, stirring constantly. Cook for about 1 minute, or until the sauce clears and thickens.

3. Stir the orange zest and juice into the hot sauce. Add the cherries and cook until heated through, 30 to 60 seconds.

4. Scoop the ice cream into 6 dessert dishes. In a small saucepan, heat the brandy until warm. Carefully ignite the brandy with a match and quickly pour it into the cherry mixture. Immediately ladle the cherry mixture over the ice cream and serve.

6 SERVINGS

CREPES SUZETTE

Pick up a package of prepared crepes at the supermarket to use in making this wonderful classic dessert. They are usually found in the produce or refrigerator sections.

1 orange
1 package (4 ounces) ready-to-use crepes (containing ten
   9-inch crepes)
6 tablespoons unsalted butter
3 tablespoons sugar
3 tablespoons orange-flavored liqueur, such as Triple Sec

1. Grate the colored zest from the orange; set aside. Cut the orange in half and squeeze the juice from both halves; reserve. Fold each crepe in half, then fold each half into quarters, making a triangle shape.

2. In a large skillet, melt the butter over medium heat. Stir in the sugar, orange zest and orange juice. Cook, stirring often, until the sugar is completely dissolved and the sauce is bubbly, 1 to 2 minutes.

3. Place the folded crepes, overlapping as necessary, in the skillet and cook, tilting the pan and spooning the sauce up over the crepes, until heated through, 1 to 2 minutes. Carefully ignite the liqueur with a match and pour the flaming liqueur over the crepes. Serve at once.

5 SERVINGS

VANILLA ICE CREAM CREPES WITH RASPBERRY COULIS

Here's an impressive dessert that uses store-bought prepared crepes. Trim the crepes a little (or fold in the sides) if they're larger than 8 inches in diameter.

6 prepared crepes, 7 to 8 inches in diameter
1½ pints rich vanilla ice cream
1½ cups raspberry dessert topping or Raspberry Coulis
(recipe follows)
Sweetened whipped cream (from a pressurized can)
6 tablespoons sliced almonds

1. If desired, heat the crepes stacked between wax paper in a microwave oven on High for 20 to 30 seconds.

2. Place 2 small scoops of ice cream down the center of each crepe. Roll up and place the filled crepes seam-side down on each of 6 dessert plates.

3. Spoon some of the raspberry dessert topping or Raspberry Coulis over the crepes. Top each with a small mound of whipped cream and 1 tablespoon of the almonds. Serve at once.

6 SERVINGS

RASPBERRY COULIS

Although some people prefer to remove the seeds from the berries, others find the effort is not worth it. Suit yourself. In either case, this is a brilliant red, intensely flavored dessert sauce that is marvelous over ice cream, fruit or pound cake.

1 package (12 ounces) thawed frozen unsweetened red
    raspberries
3 tablespoons powdered sugar
2 tablespoons kirsch or Triple Sec

1. In a food processor, combine the raspberries and powdered sugar. Process until pureed. If you want to remove the seeds, pass the sauce through a sieve.

2. Stir in the kirsch. If not using immediately, cover and refrigerate.

MAKES ABOUT 1 1/4 CUPS

RICH FLOURLESS CHOCOLATE FANTASY

When you want a sinfully rich chocolate dessert, this is a good choice. It can stand alone or place thin slices in a pool of Raspberry Coulis or melted vanilla ice cream. Or top with whipped cream.

1 package (12 ounces) semisweet or bittersweet chocolate, cut up
1 stick (4 ounces) butter
¼ cup sugar
¼ cup strong freshly brewed coffee
3 eggs

1. Preheat the oven to 425 degrees F. Butter an 8-inch springform pan. Line with a wax paper round cut to fit the bottom of the pan; butter the wax paper.

2. In a medium glass bowl, combine the chocolate, butter, sugar and coffee. Microwave on High for 1½ to 2 minutes, or until the chocolate and butter are melted and smooth when stirred.

3. Whisk in the eggs until smooth and well blended. Turn the mixture into the prepared pan.

4. Bake for 10 minutes. The cake will not be completely set in the middle. Cool to room temperature, then refrigerate until cold.

5. To serve, remove the springform. Cut the cake into thin slices; peel off wax paper as each slice is placed on the serving dish.

10 TO 12 SERVINGS

LEMON RASPBERRY TRIFLE

1 frozen all-butter pound cake (10¾ ounces)
2 pint baskets fresh raspberries
2 cups heavy cream (1 pint)
1 jar (11¼ ounces) lemon curd
½ cup Chambord liqueur or kirsch

1. If necessary, thaw the cake in a microwave oven. Rinse the raspberries and drain them on a double thickness of paper towels.

2. In a medium bowl with an electric mixer on high speed, beat the cream to soft peaks. Remove half of the whipped cream to another dish and set aside. To the whipped cream remaining in the bowl, with the mixer on low speed, beat in the lemon curd until thoroughly blended.

3. Cut the pound cake crosswise into ½-inch-thick slices. Line a 2-quart glass serving bowl with half of the cake slices, curving them partway up the sides of the bowl. Drizzle half of the Chambord over the cake. Spoon half of the lemon mixture over the cake slices and top with half of the raspberries. Cover the trifle with a single layer of the remaining cake slices. Sprinkle the cake slices with the remaining Chambord and top with the remaining lemon curd mixture.

4. Spread the reserved whipped cream evenly over the trifle and garnish the top with the remaining raspberries (they are pretty arranged in a circle around the outer edge of the dish). Serve immediately or cover and refrigerate until serving time.

8 TO 10 SERVINGS

MILE-HIGH MUD PIE

4½ ounces chocolate wafer cookies (½ of a 9-ounce box)
  3 tablespoons butter, melted
  ½ gallon coffee ice cream, softened slightly
  1 jar (about 18 ounces) chocolate fudge topping or
    chocolate almond fudge topping
  Whipped cream (optional)

1. In a food processor or blender, grind cookies to crumbs; there should be 1⅓ cups. In a medium bowl, mix together the cookie crumbs and butter. Press into the bottom and ½ inch up the sides of an 8-inch springform pan.

2. Spread half of the coffee ice cream evenly and carefully over the crumbs, smoothing the top. It's easiest and fastest to cut open the ice cream container and cut the ice cream into big pieces or slices using a large knife and then fit them into the pan.

3. Spread one-third to one-half of the fudge topping from the jar (do not heat) over the ice cream. Refrigerate the fudge topping remaining in the jar. Working quickly, carefully top with the remaining ice cream, smoothing evenly. Freeze about 2 hours, or until firm.

4. To serve, remove the sides of the springform pan. Microwave the remaining fudge topping in a microwave-safe container on High for about 45 to 60 seconds, or just until warm. Cut the ice cream pie into wedges and serve topped with some of the warm fudge topping. Garnish with whipped cream, if desired.

8 TO 10 SERVINGS

DOUBLE STRAWBERRY PIE

A bright and juicy fresh strawberry pie just like those you find at specialty shops—but this is *5 in 10* easy.

3 pint baskets fresh strawberries, chilled
1 package (4¾ ounces) strawberry-flavored junket Danish dessert pudding, pie glaze and filling mix
1 prepared 9-inch graham cracker crust
1 cup heavy cream
1 teaspoon vanilla extract

1. Rinse, dry and hull the strawberries. Set aside half of the strawberries, choosing the nicest looking ones to remain whole. Slice the remaining berries.

2. In a medium saucepan, stir the pudding and glaze mix into 1²/₃ cups cold water. Bring to a boil and boil, stirring constantly, for only 1 minute.

3. Remove from the heat and spoon a thin layer of the glaze over the bottom of the pastry shell. Place all of the sliced berries evenly in the pastry shell and top with about half of the glaze.

4. Arrange the whole berries on top (pointed end up), piling them up in the center. Spoon the remaining glaze carefully over the whole berries and in between. Refrigerate until the glaze is set. Before serving, whip the cream until stiff. Beat in the vanilla. Garnish the pie slices with plenty of whipped cream.

6 TO 8 SERVINGS

TIRAMISU

1 cup mascarpone cheese
1/2 cup heavy cream
1/3 cup powdered sugar
1/4 cup Kahlúa or other coffee-flavored liqueur mixed with
    1/4 cup very hot water
12 crisp, dry imported Italian ladyfingers (Savoiardi)

1. In a medium bowl with an electric mixer on low speed, beat together the mascarpone cheese, cream and powdered sugar until blended. Then beat on high speed until the mixture thickens somewhat, about 3 minutes.

2. Place the Kahlúa mixed with the water in a shallow dish or bowl. Cut 8 of the ladyfingers in half crosswise. Dip 2 ladyfinger pieces quickly in the liqueur and place 2 in the bottom of a stemmed balloon-shaped wineglass. Dollop a spoonful of the mascarpone cream over the ladyfingers and spread to cover. Dip 2 more ladyfinger halves and place over the cream, then top with a little more of the mascarpone mixture.

3. Repeat the procedure with the remaining ladyfinger halves, liqueur mixture and mascarpone cream in 3 more stemmed glasses.

4. Garnish each serving with 1 of the remaining 4 undipped whole ladyfingers. Serve immediately or cover and refrigerate until serving time.

4 SERVINGS

CANNOLI

The ricotta mixture can be prepared in advance, covered and refrigerated; but stuff the cannoli shells just before serving so they don't get soggy.

1½ cups part-skim ricotta cheese
  ⅓ cup powdered sugar
  3 tablespoons finely chopped candied orange peel
  ⅓ cup finely chopped semisweet or bittersweet chocolate
  6 cannoli shells (3-ounce package)

1. In a food processor, combine the ricotta cheese and powdered sugar. Process until the mixture is as smooth as possible.

2. By hand, stir in the chopped candied orange peel and chocolate until blended.

3. Using a knife or a pastry bag fitted with an open-star tip, stuff or pipe some of the ricotta mixture into each side of the cannoli shells. Sprinkle the tops of the shells with additional sifted powdered sugar. Serve immediately.

6 SERVINGS

MOCHA-FILLED CANNOLI

This mocha filling tastes yummy, and the contrast of the smooth, soft creamy filling with the crunchy cannoli is pleasing. If you can't find the cannoli shells in your supermarket, try an Italian grocery. For a change of pace, try the filling over chocolate cake or angel food cake slices.

1 cup heavy cream
1 tablespoon instant espresso powder
1/4 cup powdered sugar
1/2 cup miniature semisweet chocolate chips
6 cannoli shells (3-ounce package)

1. In a medium bowl with an electric mixer on high speed, beat the cream with the espresso powder and powdered sugar until stiff peaks form. Fold in the mini chips.

2. Fill the cannoli shells with the cream. Either pipe it or use a knife and fill the shells from both open ends. Serve immediately.

6 SERVINGS

CARAMEL-SAUCED ORANGE SLICES

Light and luxurious, the combination of orange and caramel is delightful, a perfect sweet ending to almost any meal. For an added festive touch, garnish the plates with a sprinkling of chopped macadamia nuts.

3/4 cup packed dark brown sugar
3/4 cup heavy cream
2 teaspoons butter
1 teaspoon vanilla extract or 1 tablespoon brandy
6 navel oranges

1. In a medium saucepan, combine the brown sugar and cream. Heat to boiling over high heat, whisking constantly. Reduce the heat to medium-low and simmer, uncovered, until slightly thickened, about 5 minutes. Remove from the heat. Stir in the butter and vanilla.

2. Peel the oranges and cut crosswise into 3/8-inch-thick slices or rounds. Arrange the orange slices, overlapping slightly, in a circle on 6 dessert plates.

3. Spoon some of the caramel sauce over the orange slices on each plate, dividing evenly. Serve immediately.

6 SERVINGS

PINEAPPLE JELLY-ROLL SWIRL

This looks pretty and tastes delicious. Use the prepared filled jelly rolls available in supermarket baked goods sections.

1/3 cup shredded coconut
1 package (5.1 ounces) instant vanilla pudding and pie filling mix
1 can (20 ounces) crushed pineapple packed in unsweetened juice
1 1/2 cups heavy cream
1 package (8 3/4 ounces) jelly rolls

1. Spread the coconut out on a double thickness of white paper towels. Microwave on High for 2 to 2 1/2 minutes, or until the coconut starts to turn a light golden brown. Watch carefully, because it can burn quickly.

2. Meanwhile, in a medium bowl, mix the dry pudding mix and undrained pineapple until well blended.

3. In another medium bowl with an electric mixer on high speed, beat the cream to stiff peaks. Fold in the pineapple mixture.

4. Cut the jelly rolls crosswise into 3/4-inch slices. Stand the slices up around the sides of a 9-inch springform pan. Spoon half of the pudding mixture into the pan, spreading evenly. Top with any remaining jelly-roll slices, cut-sides down. Spoon on the remaining pudding mixture, spreading evenly. Sprinkle the toasted coconut over the top. Refrigerate for 15 minutes, or until serving time.

8 SERVINGS

BROILED STRAWBERRIES BRULEE

You won't believe how good this tastes! Unfortunately, it's not for the calorie-conscious, but it's worth an occasional splurge. Substitute raspberries for the strawberries when you get a good buy on them.

4 ounces cream cheese or Neufchâtel (light) cream cheese, softened
$3/4$ cup sour cream (light, if desired)
$1/4$ cup granulated sugar
4 cups sliced fresh strawberries (about 2 pints)
$1/4$ cup packed brown sugar

1. Preheat the broiler. In a small bowl, blend together the cream cheese, sour cream and granulated sugar until smooth.

2. Place 1 cup of the berries in each of 4 shallow, 5- to 6-inch wide round ovenproof ramekins or individual gratin dishes.

3. Spoon one-fourth of the cream cheese mixture evenly over the top of the berries in each dish. Sprinkle the top of each with 1 tablespoon of the brown sugar.

4. Broil 6 inches from the heat for 3 to 3½ minutes, or until the brown sugar bubbles and caramelizes slightly. Watch carefully to avoid burning the sugar. Serve while hot.

4 SERVINGS

BAKED BRIE WITH APRICOTS AND ALMONDS

In some European countries, fruit and cheese for dessert is commonplace. This variation on the theme has a sweet twist.

1 wheel (2.2 pounds) Brie cheese, rind left on (see Note)
1/2 cup apricot or apricot-pineapple preserves, at room temperature
1/2 cup chopped dried apricots
1/3 cup sliced almonds
French bread slices, warmed, or crackers or slices of fresh fruit, such as apples, pears, nectarines or peaches

1. Preheat the oven to 350 degrees F. Place the Brie in a round ovenproof serving dish (such as a decorative pie plate or quiche dish) that it exactly fits into with no extra space around the sides.

2. In a small bowl, mix together the apricot preserves and dried apricots. Spread evenly over the Brie. Sprinkle the almonds evenly over the top.

3. Bake 7 to 8 minutes, or just until heated through. Serve immediately with warm bread, crackers or fruit.

10 TO 12 SERVINGS

NOTE: If a wheel of Brie is not available, buy an equivalent amount of Brie in two wedges and position in a tight-fitting ovenproof serving dish to look like a round, cutting a little if necessary. The recipe can be halved to make fewer servings, in which case the Brie may require a few minutes less baking time.

STRAWBERRY CHOCOLATE TRUFFLE PIZZA

This dessert is a showstopper. Although you'll have to work quickly to prepare this within 10 minutes, if you whip it up and refrigerate it before dinner, it will be ready by dessert time.

1 roll or package (20 ounces) refrigerated sugar cookie
    dough
1 cup semisweet chocolate chips (6 ounces)
1/4 cup heavy cream
1/2 teaspoon vanilla extract
2 pint baskets fresh strawberries

1. Preheat the oven to 400 degrees F. Cut the cookie dough into 1/4-inch slices. Place in a foil-lined 14-inch round pizza pan with a 1/2-inch high rim. Press together to form a crust on the bottom. Bake for 8 to 9 minutes, or until golden.

2. Meanwhile, in a 2-cup glass measure, combine the chocolate chips and cream. Microwave on High for 1 1/2 minutes, or until the chocolate is melted and smooth when stirred. Stir in the vanilla.

3. Rinse, drain and hull the strawberries. Cut in half lengthwise.

4. Spread the chocolate cream evenly over the baked crust. Beginning at the edge, arrange the strawberries on the "pizza" in concentric circles, cut-sides down and with the points toward the outside edge of the pan; cover the chocolate completely with berries. Refrigerate until set, at least 20 to 30 minutes.

12 TO 16 SERVINGS

2 Cakes, Pies and Tarts

While 10 minutes doesn't allow time for baking cakes or pies from scratch, it's still possible to turn out delectable desserts with a little help from store-bought cakes and crumb-style crusts. Frozen all-butter pound cakes, prepared chocolate loaf cakes (from the baked goods sections of supermarkets) and prepared angel food cakes are all wonderful timesavers.

Layer a pound cake with vanilla pudding and top with chocolate glaze for an instant Boston Cream Pie. Or use a loaf cake to make an Italian Cassata filled with ricotta cheese, Grand Marnier, candied orange peel and finely chopped chocolate. Angel food cake lends itself to a cream cheese mixture that is topped with cherry pie filling.

And if you love strawberry shortcake, try this version using cookies instead of those rubbery store-bought spongelike cakes. It's a winner! Or prepared Nectarine Shortcake with pound cake slices, Triple Sec, cream, raspberry jam and nectarines. No one will believe it's a *5 in 10* dessert.

If you have a penchant for pie, prepared crusts are another lifesaver. You'll find ready-to-bake pastry, all rolled out, in the refrigerated section of your supermarket. Graham cracker and ready-to-serve chocolate and vanilla wafer cookie crumb crusts are usually on the shelf in the baking section.

QUICK APRICOT SNACK CAKE

When you want a cake in minutes, whip out this creation with a little help from buttermilk baking mix and the microwave oven. To vary the flavor of this cake, an equal amount of other chopped dried fruits or chocolate chips can be substituted for the apricots.

2 cups buttermilk baking mix, such as Bisquick
1/3 cup plus 1 tablespoon sugar
2 eggs
2/3 cup chopped dried apricots
1/2 teaspoon cinnamon

1. In a medium bowl with an electric mixer on medium speed, beat together the baking mix, 1/3 cup of the sugar, the eggs and 1/2 cup of cold water until well blended, 1 to 1 1/2 minutes. Stir in the chopped dried apricots.

2. Spread the batter evenly in a well-greased 8-inch square glass baking dish.

3. Microwave on High for 4 minutes, turning once.

4. Stir together the cinnamon and remaining 1 tablespoon sugar and sprinkle evenly over the top of the cake. Microwave on High 1 to 2 minutes longer, turning once, until a toothpick inserted in the center comes out clean (there may be a few wet looking spots on top, but that's fine). Let cool, then cut into pieces.

BOSTON CREAM PIE

You can make this loaf variation on the classic layer cake in minutes, with a little help from convenience foods. This recipe uses less liquid than the pudding and pie filling mix calls for, so be sure to follow the instructions below, rather than on the package.

1 package (3.4 ounces) instant vanilla or French vanilla pudding and pie filling mix
1 cup milk
1/2 cup semisweet chocolate chips
1 frozen all-butter pound cake (10³/₄ ounces), thawed

1. In a medium bowl, whisk together the pudding mix and milk for 1 to 2 minutes, or until the pudding starts to thicken. Let stand while preparing the cake.

2. In a glass measure or dish, combine the chocolate chips and 1½ tablespoons of water. Microwave on High for 35 to 45 seconds, until the chocolate is melted and smooth when stirred.

3. Slice the pound cake horizontally into 3 equal layers. Place the bottom layer on a serving plate. Spread half of the pudding mixture evenly over the cake. Cover with the middle cake layer. Spread evenly with the remaining pudding mixture and top with the remaining cake layer.

4. Spread the chocolate evenly over the top, allowing some of it to drip down the sides, if possible. Serve immediately or refrigerate. Cut into slices with a large serrated knife.

6 TO 8 SERVINGS

ITALIAN CASSATA

This is a streamlined version of the classic dessert. To spruce it up, serve the slices drizzled with hot fudge sauce. An all-butter pound cake can be used in place of the chocolate loaf cake, if you prefer.

1 container (15 ounces) whole-milk ricotta cheese
3 tablespoons Grand Marnier or orange juice
1/2 cup finely chopped candied orange peel
1/2 cup finely chopped bittersweet or semisweet chocolate
1 prepared chocolate loaf cake (15 ounces)

1. In a medium bowl, mix together the ricotta cheese, Grand Marnier, orange peel and chocolate until blended.

2. Cut the loaf cake horizontally into 3 equal layers. Place the bottom cake layer on a serving plate. Spread one-third of the ricotta filling over the cake. Top with the second cake layer and spread with half of the remaining ricotta. Top with the last cake layer and spread the remaining ricotta filling on top.

3. Serve immediately or refrigerate until serving time. To serve, carefully cut the cake into slices and place the slices, cut-sides down, on plates.

10 TO 12 SERVINGS

MINI CHEESECAKES

For cheesecake fanciers, whip up a batch of these on short notice. Top with canned cherry, blueberry or peach pie filling.

15 chocolate wafer cookies
2 packages (8 ounces each) cream cheese, softened
2/3 cup sugar
2 eggs
1 can (21 ounces) red ruby cherry pie filling or topping

1. Preheat the oven to 450 degrees F. Line 15 (2¾-inch) muffin cups with laminated foil liners. With your fingers, crumble a cookie into the bottom of each muffin cup.

2. In a medium bowl, beat together the cream cheese, sugar and eggs until smooth. Spoon some of the cream cheese mixture over the cookie crumbs in each muffin cup, filling them about ⅔ full.

3. Place in the oven and immediately reduce the oven temperature to 425 degrees F. Bake for 9 to 10 minutes, or until set. Remove from the oven and let stand until cooled.

4. Top each cheesecake with some of the cherry pie topping, dividing evenly. Refrigerate 30 to 60 minutes, or until serving time.

MAKES 15 CUPCAKE-SIZE CHEESECAKES

CHOCOLATE-GRAND MARNIER POUND CAKE

When you need to turn a store-bought pound cake into something special, nothing does the trick better than chocolate butter frosting.

1 frozen all-butter pound cake (10¾ ounces)
8 tablespoons (1 stick) unsalted butter, softened
2 cups powdered sugar
½ cup unsweetened cocoa powder
¼ cup Grand Marnier or orange juice

1. Thaw the pound cake in a microwave oven if necessary. Split the cake into 3 equal horizontal layers.

2. In a medium bowl with an electric mixer on medium speed, beat together the butter, powdered sugar, cocoa and Grand Marnier until smooth and fluffy.

3. Place the bottom cake layer on a serving plate. Spread about one-fourth frosting over the cake. Top with the middle layer and spread with one-third of the remaining frosting. Top with the middle layer and spread with one-third of the remaining frosting. Cover with the top cake layer and frost the top and the sides with the remaining chocolate frosting. Cut into slices and serve or refrigerate until serving time.

6 TO 8 SERVINGS

CHOCOLATE HAZELNUT TORTE WITH FRESH STRAWBERRIES

This is the ultimate quick torte, made by spreading prepared creamy chocolate hazelnut spread between pound cake layers and topping with fresh strawberries. Dessert doesn't get much easier. If you don't have berries on hand, top the cake with chopped blanched almonds or even toasted pecans.

1 pint basket fresh strawberries
1 frozen all-butter pound cake (10¾ ounces)
¾ cup chocolate creamy hazelnut spread (such as Nutella)

1. Rinse, dry, hull and slice the strawberries. If necessary, thaw cake in microwave according to package directions.

2. Cut the cake horizontally into 3 equal layers. Place the bottom cake layer on a serving plate. Spread evenly with a thin layer of the hazelnut spread. Top with the middle cake layer and spread with another layer of the hazelnut spread. Top with the remaining cake layer and frost the top and the sides of the cake with the remaining hazelnut spread.

3. Top the cake with rows of overlapping strawberry slices. To serve, cut the cake into slices and serve immediately with any remaining berries.

8 TO 10 SERVINGS

CHOCOLATE-FROSTED ANGEL CAKE

Here's an easy way to make a high, light and handsome chocolate-frosted cake in no time.

1 package (12 ounces) semisweet chocolate chips
4 tablespoons butter, cut up
3 tablespoons light corn syrup
²/₃ cup powdered sugar
1 angel food cake (1 pound)

1. In a medium glass bowl or 1-quart glass measure, combine the chocolate chips, butter, corn syrup and 2 tablespoons water. Microwave on High for 1½ to 1¾ minutes, or until the chocolate is melted and smooth when stirred.

2. Sift the powdered sugar into the chocolate, stirring until well blended. Cool 5 minutes.

3. Split the cake in half horizontally so you end up with 2 equal layers. Place the bottom cake layer on a serving plate. Spread about one-third of the frosting evenly over the bottom layer. Cover with the top cake layer. Spread the remaining frosting over the top and sides of the cake. Refrigerate until serving time.

10 SERVINGS

CHERRY ANGEL SQUARES

This is also delicious topped with peach pie filling instead of cherry.

1 angel food cake (12 ounces)
1 cup heavy cream
1 package (8 ounces) cream cheese, softened
1 cup powdered sugar
1 can (20 ounces) light cherry pie filling or topping, chilled

1. Cut the cake into 1-inch cubes. There should be about 8 cups.

1. In a medium bowl with an electric mixer on high speed, beat the cream until soft peaks form.

2. In a large bowl, beat together the cream cheese and powdered sugar until smooth. Stir in one-fourth of the whipped cream to lighten the cheese. Fold into the remaining whipped cream until thoroughly blended.

3. Add the cake cubes and fold until well mixed. Turn into a 7-by-11-inch baking dish, spreading evenly and smoothing the top.

4. Spread the chilled pie topping evenly over the top. Refrigerate until serving time. Cut into squares to serve.

8 SERVINGS

NECTARINE SHORTCAKE

Peaches or strawberries can be substituted for the nectarines. If time is really short, forgo whipping the cream and rely on sweetened whipped cream in a can from the supermarket.

> 1 frozen all-butter pound cake (10¾ ounces)
> 8 nectarines
> 2 to 3 tablespoons Triple Sec, Chambord or orange juice
> 1½ cups heavy cream
> 8 teaspoons seedless red raspberry jam or peach preserves

1. Thaw the pound cake in a microwave if necessary. Cut the cake crosswise into 8 slices.

2. Cut the unpeeled nectarines into slices or chunks, discarding the pits. Place the fruit in a medium bowl. Stir in the Triple Sec until well mixed.

3. In a medium bowl with an electric mixer on high speed, beat the cream to stiff peaks.

4. To assemble the dessert, place a cake slice on each of 8 plates. Spread 1 teaspoon raspberry jam over each slice of cake. Top with a little whipped cream and then with some of the nectarine mixture, dividing evenly. Dollop the remaining whipped cream on top.

8 SERVINGS

STRAWBERRY COOKIECAKE

This is a fast and delicious way to make strawberry shortcake during strawberry season—use cookies for the base instead of cake. It's a favorite at our house.

2 pint baskets fresh strawberries
2 tablespoons granulated sugar
1 cup heavy cream
1 to 2 tablespoons powdered sugar
12 Brussels cookies or Geneva cookies (layered with
    chocolate and pecans) or shortbread cookies

1. Rinse, drain and hull the strawberries. Reserve 6 large berries. Slice the remaining strawberries into a bowl and toss with the granulated sugar. Let stand a few minutes.

2. Meanwhile, in a medium bowl with an electric mixer on high speed, beat the cream with the powdered sugar to stiff peaks.

3. To assemble the dessert, place 2 cookies on each of 6 dessert plates. Stand 1 whole strawberry, pointed end up, in the center of the 2 cookies on each plate. Surround with the sliced berries.

4. Top the sliced berries with dollops of the whipped cream. Serve immediately.

6 SERVINGS

LAYERED STRAWBERRIES AND CREAM CAKE

Vary the flavor of this dessert by choosing graham cracker, shortbread or chocolate wafer cookie crumbs in place of the vanilla. As a substitute for the strawberries, try raspberries, boysenberries or blueberries in season. If not serving immediately, keep refrigerated.

1 cup vanilla wafer cookie crumbs
1¼ cups heavy cream
8 tablespoons (1 stick) butter, softened
1½ cups powdered sugar
1 pint basket fresh strawberries

1. Sprinkle a generous ½ cup of the cookie crumbs evenly over the bottom of an 8-inch square baking pan. In a medium bowl with an electric mixer on high speed, beat 1 cup of the cream to stiff peaks.

2. In another medium bowl with the electric mixer on medium speed, beat together the butter, powdered sugar and remaining ¼ cup cream until smooth and fluffy. Carefully drop spoonfuls of the butter mixture over the crumbs. Spread evenly with a knife. Refrigerate for a few minutes.

3. Meanwhile rinse, drain, hull and slice the strawberries. Arrange the strawberry slices evenly on top of the butter mixture. Cover with all of the whipped cream and sprinkle the remaining cookie crumbs on top. To serve, carefully cut into 9 pieces and gently lift out, a piece at a time, with a metal spatula.

9 SERVINGS

BLACK AND WHITE
ICE CREAM CAKE

Once you've assembled this easy dessert, let the freezer do the rest. Vary the ice cream flavors according to your personal taste.

> 1 large frozen all-butter pound cake (16 ounces)
> About ½ cup coffee-, orange- or raspberry-flavored liqueur
> 1 quart chocolate or chocolate fudge ice cream, softened slightly
> Sweetened whipped cream (from a pressurized can)
> Bittersweet chocolate

1. If the pound cake is still frozen, thaw it in the microwave for a minute or two. Cut the cake crosswise into ½-inch slices.

2. Line an 8-inch square pan with 2 sheets of plastic wrap, allowing plenty of overlap in both directions. Place a layer of the pound cake slices (cutting as necessary to fit) in the bottom of the lined pan. Sprinkle about ¼ cup of the liqueur over the cake slices.

3. Spread half of the softened chocolate ice cream evenly on top. Repeat the layers, ending with the ice cream. Bring the plastic wrap extending over the sides of the pan up over the ice cream. Cover tightly with foil. Freeze until firm, 3 to 4 hours or overnight.

4. To serve, cut the ice cream cake into squares and garnish with a swirl of whipped cream. Grate a bit of chocolate decoratively on top.

8 TO 9 SERVINGS

INDIVIDUAL OPEN-FACE APPLE PIES

1 can (21 ounces) apple pie filling or topping
3/4 teaspoon ground cinnamon
4 tablespoons unsalted butter
4 filo dough sheets, each about 13 by 17 inches
1/3 cup sliced almonds

1. Preheat the oven to 375 degrees F. In a medium bowl, mix together the apple pie filling and the cinnamon. Place the butter in a small glass bowl or cup. Microwave on High 40 to 45 seconds, or until melted.

2. Unwrap the filo dough and place on a large sheet of wax paper. Cover with wax paper and a damp towel; remove the sheets of dough only as you need them. On another large sheet of wax paper, stack the filo sheets, brushing each with butter to cover before adding the next. Brush the top layer with butter.

3. With a sharp knife, cut the filo into 12 squares, each about 4 inches. Press 1 filo dough square into each of 12 ungreased muffin cups (2 3/4 inches in diameter), with the edges of the filo extending up over the rims of the cups.

4. Fill with the apple mixture, dividing evenly. Sprinkle the almonds on top. Brush the edges of the dough with any remaining melted butter. Bake about 10 minutes, or until the filo is a rich golden brown. Remove from the oven. Cool 5 minutes, then serve.

12 SERVINGS

CHOCOLATE EGGNOG PIE

This is a terrific holiday offering when you have plenty of eggnog in the fridge.

1 package (3.4 ounces) instant vanilla flavor pudding and
  pie filling mix
1⅓ cups commercial eggnog
1 cup heavy cream
1 cup finely chopped bittersweet chocolate
1 prepared 8-inch chocolate crumb crust

1. In a medium bowl, whisk together the pudding mix and eggnog for 1 to 2 minutes, or until the mixture is well blended and smooth.

2. In a medium bowl with an electric mixer on high speed, beat the cream to stiff peaks. Fold the whipped cream into the pudding mixture until thoroughly blended.

3. Stir in ¾ cup of the chocolate. Turn the filling into the crust.

4. Garnish the top with the remaining ¼ cup chocolate. Refrigerate until serving time, ½ hour or longer. To serve, cut into slices.

6 TO 8 SERVINGS

FRUITED CREAM CHEESE PIE

Embellish this no-bake dessert with beautiful fresh fruit. When your favorites are out of season, top with a can of chilled cherry pie filling.

  1 small package (3 ounces) cream cheese, softened
$1/2$ cup powdered sugar
  1 cup heavy cream
  1 prepared 8-inch vanilla wafer crumb crust
    Fresh nectarine or peach slices, grapes and/or raspberries

1. Beat together the cream cheese and powdered sugar until smooth.

2. In a medium bowl with an electric mixer, beat the cream to stiff peaks. Gently fold the whipped cream into the sweetened cream cheese. Turn into the prepared crust, spreading evenly.

3. Top with an attractive arrangement of fresh fruit. Refrigerate 1 to 2 hours, or until serving time.

6 SERVINGS

KAHLUA PIE

Here's a rich, silky pie coffee lovers will relish. It's fine on its own, topped with a dollop of whipped cream or sprinkled with chopped chocolate or nuts.

1 refrigerated all-ready 9-inch pie crust
1 envelope unflavored gelatin
$^1/_3$ cup Kahlúa or other coffee-flavored liqueur
2 cups heavy cream
$^1/_3$ cup sugar

1. Preheat the oven to 450 degrees F. Fit pastry into a 9-inch metal pie pan. Bake until pale golden, about 10 minutes.

2. Meanwhile, sprinkle the gelatin on $^1/_3$ cup cold water in a small glass bowl or measure. Let stand 1 minute to soften. Microwave on High 1 minute; stir to dissolve the gelatin. Stir in the Kahlúa and set aside to cool (put in freezer for 5 minutes, if desired, to speed cooling).

3. Meanwhile, in a large bowl with an electric mixer on high speed, beat the cream with the sugar until stiff. Fold in the cool gelatin, mixing until thoroughly blended.

4. Turn into the pastry crust. Refrigerate until set, about 2 hours, or overnight.

6 TO 8 SERVINGS

PEANUT BUTTER-CREAM CHEESE PIE

This is great to stash in the freezer, ready to serve on a moment's notice. Serve slices "as is" or gussy them up by topping with hot fudge sauce warmed in the microwave.

1 cup heavy cream
1 package (8 ounces) cream cheese, softened
1 cup powdered sugar
1/2 cup chunky peanut butter
1 prepared 8-inch chocolate crumb crust

1. In a medium bowl with an electric mixer on high speed, beat the cream until stiff peaks form.

2. Using another medium bowl and the same beaters on low speed, beat together the cream cheese, powdered sugar and peanut butter until well blended.

3. Beat in half of the whipped cream until blended. Fold in the remaining whipped cream until well blended.

4. Turn the mixture into the crumb crust. Cover and freeze 1 hour or longer.

6 TO 8 SERVINGS

PECAN TART

Drizzle a little melted white or bittersweet chocolate over the tart before chilling for an appealing look. Cut the slices small as this is rich.

1 refrigerated all-ready 9-inch pie crust
2 cups pecan halves
2/3 cup packed light brown sugar
1/3 cup heavy cream
2 tablespoons butter

1. Preheat the oven to 450 degrees F. Meanwhile, remove the pie crust from the refrigerator and let it stand at room temperature for 10 minutes.

2. Unfold the crust, remove the top plastic sheet and press out the fold lines, spreading the crust out with your fingers. Place the crust in a 9½-inch fluted tart pan with a removable bottom. Remove the second plastic sheet and ease the crust into the pan, pressing firmly against the bottom and sides. Fold under the edge of the crust along the top edge of the pan so the crust is even with it.

3. Arrange the pecans evenly over the crust. In a large skillet, combine the brown sugar, cream and butter. Bring to a boil over medium-high heat, stirring often. Boil 1 minute to thicken slightly. Pour evenly over the pecans in the pie shell.

4. Bake for 8 to 9 minutes, or until the filling is bubbly, checking once to make sure the nuts are not overbrowning. Cool to room temperature or serve slightly warm.

10 TO 12 SERVINGS

FLUFFY FREEZER PUMPKIN PIE

Make this several hours in advance of serving and freeze. For another variation, omit the pie crust and spoon the pumpkin filling on top of crushed gingersnap cookies in stemmed dessert glasses; serve immediately.

½ of a 30-ounce can pumpkin pie filling with spices included (about 1½ cups)
1 container (8 ounces) frozen extra creamy whipped topping with real whipped cream, thawed
1 prepared 8-inch butter-flavored or graham cracker crust
⅔ cup coarsely chopped pecans

1. In a medium bowl, fold together the pumpkin pie filling and thawed whipped topping until thoroughly blended and no white streaks remain.

2. Scrape the filling into the crust, spreading evenly. Sprinkle the pecans evenly over the top.

3. Cover and freeze until firm, 2 hours or longer. Let soften 5 to 10 minutes before cutting into slices and serving.

6 TO 8 SERVINGS

No-Bake Pumpkin Pie

When you need a hassle-free holiday pie fast, rely on this recipe. For extra texture, sprinkle coarsely chopped pecans over the top.

1 cup heavy cream
1 package (3.4 ounces) instant vanilla or French vanilla pudding and pie filling mix
$\frac{1}{2}$ cup milk
1 cup canned pumpkin pie mix (with spices included)
1 prepared 8-inch graham cracker crust

1. In a medium bowl with an electric mixer on high speed, beat the cream to stiff peaks.

2. In another medium bowl, whisk together the pudding mix and milk for 1 to 2 minutes, until smooth and well blended. Whisk in the pumpkin until thoroughly blended.

3. Fold in the whipped cream until no white streaks remain. Turn into the crust, spreading evenly.

4. Refrigerate until serving time, 1 to 2 hours or longer. To serve, cut into slices.

6 TO 8 SERVINGS

FLUFFY BLUEBERRY YOGURT PIE

Keep this easy pie stashed in the freezer to pull out on a moment's notice or toss it together at the last moment if you have unexpected guests. It's especially appealing during the warm weather months when you don't want to heat up the kitchen.

2 cups fresh or frozen (do not thaw) unsweetened blueberries
1 container (8 ounces) blueberry yogurt
1 container (8 ounces) frozen whipped topping, thawed
1/2 teaspoon vanilla extract
1 prepared 8-inch graham cracker or vanilla wafer crumb crust

1. If the blueberries are fresh, rinse and drain them. Set on paper towels to dry. Leave frozen berries in the freezer.

2. In a medium bowl, combine the yogurt, whipped topping and vanilla. Whisk to blend well.

3. Fold 1 cup of the fresh or frozen blueberries into the yogurt mixture. Turn into the crust, spreading evenly. Freeze until firm, 1 to 2 hours.

4. Remove the pie from the freezer about 30 minutes before serving to allow the pie to soften slightly. If using frozen berries, remove them from the freezer at this point. To serve, cut into wedges. Garnish with the remaining 1 cup blueberries.

6 TO 8 SERVINGS

FROZEN YOGURT FRUIT PIE

This recipe is versatile. Vary the yogurt flavor according to the frozen fruit (try raspberries, strawberries, etc.) you plan to use.

4 ounces cream cheese, softened
1 container (8 ounces) peach, raspberry or strawberry-banana
 yogurt
1 container (8 ounces) frozen extra creamy whipped topping
 with real cream, thawed
1 bag (16 ounces) frozen sliced peaches
1 prepared graham cracker crumb crust (8 inches in diameter)

1. In a medium bowl, mix together the cream cheese and yogurt until smooth. Whisk in the thawed topping until well blended.

2. Chop up enough of the frozen peaches (do not thaw) to make $1\frac{1}{2}$ cups. Fold the chopped frozen peaches into the yogurt mixture.

3. Scrape the peach-yogurt filling into the crust. Arrange the remaining frozen peach slices attractively on top.

4. Cover the pie with plastic wrap and freeze 2 to 3 hours, or until firm. Remove from the freezer 10 minutes before cutting into slices and serving.

8 SERVINGS

Almond Peach Tart

Almond paste fanciers will love the sophistication and flavor of this fresh fruit tart.

1 refrigerated all-ready 9-inch pie crust
1 can (29 ounces) sliced peaches
1 package (7 ounces) almond paste
1 egg
1/3 cup apricot preserves

1. Remove the pie crust from the refrigerator and let it stand at room temperature for 10 minutes. Meanwhile, preheat the oven to 450 degrees F. Drain the peaches and set on paper towels to dry.

2. In a food processor, process the almond paste with the egg until well blended.

3. Unfold the crust, remove the top plastic sheet and press out the fold lines. Place the crust in a buttered 9½-inch fluted tart pan with removable bottom. Remove the second plastic sheet. Spread the almond mixture evenly over the crust.

4. Bake 9 to 10 minutes, or until the top and crust are golden brown. Set aside to cool for 10 to 15 minutes.

5. Meanwhile, place the apricot preserves in a glass dish. Microwave on High for 30 to 40 seconds, or until melted. Arrange the peach slices decoratively on top of the tart and brush the preserves over the fruit to glaze. Chill until serving time.

8 SERVINGS

JEWELED FRUIT TARTS

Vary the fruit on top of these jewel-like mini tarts for a beautiful look. Besides strawberries, try raspberries, kiwifruit, grapes and the like.

1/4 cup semisweet chocolate chips
6 prepared individual graham cracker crumb crusts
(3 1/2 inches in diameter)
1 container (8 ounces) whipped cream cheese
4 1/2 tablespoons apricot preserves
1 pint basket fresh strawberries

1. In a small glass container, microwave the chocolate chips on High for about 1 minute, or until melted and smooth when stirred. Carefully spread about 3/4 tablespoon of the melted chocolate in the bottom of each graham cracker crumb crust. Refrigerate for a few minutes to allow the chocolate to set up.

2. Meanwhile, in a small bowl, mix together the cream cheese and 1 1/2 tablespoons of the apricot preserves until blended. Rinse, drain and hull the strawberries.

3. Spoon the apricot cream cheese into the chocolate-lined crusts. Arrange 3 or 4 strawberries, pointed ends up, on top of each tart.

4. Place the remaining 3 tablespoons apricot preserves in a glass cup. Microwave on High for 20 to 30 seconds, or just until warm and spreadable. Brush the warm preserves over and around the strawberries. Serve immediately or refrigerate until serving time.

6 SERVINGS

3 PUDDINGS, CREAMS AND MOUSSES

This chapter is filled with comforting, old-fashioned, homespun desserts that bring back fond memories of childhood. These sweets are the kind of easy-to-eat treats that soothe the spirit and the mind. Puddings, mousses and creams are enjoying newfound popularity these days as cooks return to the basics with renewed interest in learning how to make them.

There's really no complicated trick to preparing these updated classics. You can whip up a downright delicious Homemade Chocolate Pudding effortlessly in a single pan on top of the stove with a little cornstarch, sugar, milk and unsweetened chocolate. After cooking, vanilla is stirred in for added flavor. Another favorite dish that serves up nostalgia is rice pudding. The shortcut version offered here is also prepared on the stove top in a jiffy with leftover cooked rice and a little orange juice and orange zest. The flavor is outstanding, and you trim the standard lengthy baking time.

Other unpretentious, tempting possibilities include Raspberry Mousse, Southern-Style Banana Pudding, Holiday Eggnog Tapioca, Strawberry Pineapple Cloud and Mocha Mousse. Use the electric mixer, food processor or microwave for ease and to speed up preparation time.

HOMEMADE CHOCOLATE PUDDING

This goes together in a jiffy and beats the taste of the packaged mixes. Be sure to use whole milk for best results. If you prefer a little crunch in your pudding, 1/4 cup chopped pecans can be added in place of the vanilla.

1/2 cup sugar
2 tablespoons cornstarch
2 cups milk
2 squares (1 ounce each) unsweetened chocolate
1 teaspoon vanilla extract

1. In a 2-quart saucepan, whisk together the sugar and cornstarch until well blended. Whisk in the milk until the mixture is thoroughly blended and the cornstarch is dissolved.

2. Coarsely chop the chocolate with a large knife or in a food processor; add to the saucepan. Cook over medium to medium-high heat, whisking constantly, until the mixture boils and thickens and the chocolate is melted and smooth, 5 to 7 minutes total.

3. Remove from the heat and stir in the vanilla. Pour into 4 dessert dishes. Serve warm or cover with plastic wrap and refrigerate until cold.

4 SERVINGS

HOMEMADE VANILLA PUDDING

3 tablespoons cornstarch
1/3 cup sugar
2 cups whole milk
1 egg
2 teaspoons vanilla extract

1. In a 2-quart saucepan, whisk together the cornstarch and sugar until well blended. Whisk in the milk until it is thoroughly blended and the cornstarch is dissolved. Cook over medium-high heat, whisking constantly, until the mixture boils and thickens, 4 to 6 minutes. Reduce the heat to medium-low.

2. In a small bowl, beat the egg. Quickly whisk about 1/4 cup of the hot milk mixture into the egg; then whisk in another 1/4 cup. Quickly whisk all of the egg mixture back into the pan.

3. Cook over medium-low heat, whisking constantly, until the pudding reaches a temperature of 165 degrees F. on a candy thermometer, 1 to 2 minutes.

4. Immediately remove from the heat and stir in the vanilla. Pour the pudding into 4 dessert dishes or custard cups. Cover with plastic wrap and refrigerate until serving time.

4 SERVINGS

MAPLE PUDDING: Prepare Homemade Vanilla Pudding as directed above, but substitute 3 tablespoons pure maple syrup for the vanilla.

SOUTHERN-STYLE BANANA PUDDING

This is best left in the fridge awhile before serving to allow the cookies to soften up a bit.

1 package (5.1 ounces) instant banana cream pudding and pie filling mix
2¾ cups milk
27 to 30 vanilla wafer cookies
5 bananas
½ cup heavy cream

1. In a medium bowl, whisk together the pudding mix and milk until the pudding starts to thicken, 1 to 2 minutes.

2. Spread a small amount of the pudding over the bottom of a 1½-quart casserole dish. Cover with a single layer of the cookies, using about 9 or 10 cookies. Peel and slice the bananas and add a layer of banana slices. Spread about ⅓ of the pudding over the bananas. Continue to layer the cookies, banana slices and pudding, making 2 more layers of each, and ending with the last of the pudding. Cover with plastic wrap and refrigerate 1 to 2 hours or overnight to chill and allow the cookies to soften.

3. Just before serving, in a medium bowl with an electric mixer, beat the cream to stiff peaks. Spread over the pudding mixture. Garnish with additional banana slices, if desired.

6 TO 8 SERVINGS

Chocolate Raisin Bread Pudding

Make the chocolate pudding first in the microwave oven; then mix in cubes of raisin bread for instant bread pudding. No baking is required. Accompany with a bowl of whipped cream to dollop on top if you like.

2 tablespoons cornstarch
2¹/₃ cups milk
1¹/₂ cups semisweet chocolate chips (9 ounces)
    4 or 5 slices cinnamon raisin bread, cut into 1-inch cubes
    ¹/₃ cup chopped pecans

1. In a 2-quart glass bowl, mix together the cornstarch and milk with a wire whisk until the cornstarch is thoroughly mixed. Add 1 cup of the chocolate chips.

2. Microwave on High for 3 minutes; whisk to mix. Microwave another 3 minutes and whisk again. Microwave for 2 to 3 minutes longer, or until the mixture is bubbly, smooth and thickened.

3. Stir in the bread cubes. Turn the pudding into an 8-inch square or 11-by-7-inch baking dish. Or divide evenly among 5 or 6 dessert dishes.

4. Sprinkle the pecans and the remaining ¹/₂ cup chocolate chips over the bread pudding. Serve immediately while warm or let cool to room temperature. Refrigerate any leftovers; reheat for a minute in the microwave oven before serving, if desired.

5 to 6 servings

MOCHA MOUSSE

Mocha here signifies chocolate and coffee. Whip this up and serve immediately or let it relax in the refrigerator until dessert time. Garnish with candy coffee beans, if you have them, or simply a pouff of whipped cream.

1 cup heavy cream
1 package (8 ounces) cream cheese, softened
3/4 cup sugar
1/4 cup unsweetened cocoa powder
1 1/2 to 2 teaspoons instant espresso powder

1. In a medium bowl with an electric mixer on high speed, beat the cream to stiff peaks. If you're using a stationary mixer, scrape the whipped cream into another bowl.

2. In the same mixer bowl with the same beaters (it's not necessary to wash either), beat the cream cheese and sugar together on medium speed until smooth. With the mixer on low speed, beat in the cocoa powder and espresso powder until well blended. Gently beat in half of the whipped cream.

3. Remove the mixer and fold in the remaining whipped cream by hand. Turn the mousse into 6 dessert dishes. Serve immediately or refrigerate until serving time.

6 SERVINGS

CHOCOLATE ORANGE MOUSSE: Prepare the Mocha Mousse as directed above, but substitute 1 tablespoon grated orange zest in place of the espresso powder.

CUSTARD-SAUCED ORANGES

Team cool orange slices with hot custard sauce for a lovely light dessert.

6 navel oranges
1½ ounces semisweet chocolate (1½ squares)
1 package (3⅛ ounces) vanilla pudding and pie filling mix (NOT instant)
2¼ cups half-and-half

1. Grate enough colored zest from 1 or 2 of the oranges to equal 1 tablespoon. Peel the oranges and cut crosswise into ½-inch-thick rounds; remove the center pith. Grate or chop the chocolate.

2. In a 1½-quart deep glass container or measure, whisk together the pudding mix and half-and-half until well blended. Microwave on High for 3 minutes; then whisk or stir well. Microwave on High for 2 minutes longer; whisk again. Microwave for 1 minute more, or until bubbly. Stir the orange zest into the custard.

3. Place about 2 tablespoons of the hot custard on each of 6 dessert plates, swirling around to cover the bottom of the plate. Arrange the orange slices, overlapping, in a circle on top of the custard. Top with the remaining custard sauce, dividing evenly.

4. Sprinkle about ½ tablespoon of the grated chocolate over each dessert. Serve immediately.

6 SERVINGS

SHERRIED PEACH PARFAITS

Try this dessert with fresh peaches when they are in season. To save time, sweetened whipped cream from a refrigerated pressurized can will be fine here. To dress up this elegant dessert even further, garnish with a generous sprinkling of nutmeg.

1½ cups milk (nonfat is fine)
  1 package (3.4 ounces) instant lemon pudding and
    pie filling mix
1½ tablespoons medium-dry or cream sherry
  1 can (29 ounces) sliced peaches, well drained
    Sweetened whipped cream

1. In a medium bowl, combine the milk and the pudding mix. Whisk 1 to 2 minutes, until very well blended. Whisk in the sherry.

2. Fold in the sliced peaches. Turn into 6 parfait glasses or dessert dishes. Let stand 5 minutes.

3. Serve topped with the whipped cream, or refrigerate until serving time.

6 SERVINGS

RASPBERRY MOUSSE

Make this dessert and serve immediately. Or refrigerate or freeze to serve later. Garnish the top with white chocolate curls or a sprinkling of sliced almonds, if you like.

1 cup heavy cream
1 package (12 ounces) frozen unsweetened raspberries
1 package (8 ounces) cream cheese, softened
1/3 to 1/2 cup powdered sugar
1/2 teaspoon vanilla extract

1. In a medium bowl with an electric mixer on high speed, beat the cream to stiff peaks.

2. In a food processor fitted with a metal blade, process the frozen berries until they are in fine pieces.

3. Cut up the softened cream cheese and add to the berries. Add 1/3 cup of the powdered sugar and the vanilla. Process until the mixture is thoroughly blended and no white remains. Taste and add more of the powdered sugar if needed.

4. Turn into a medium bowl and fold in the whipped cream. Spoon the mousse into 5 or 6 dessert serving dishes or stemmed goblets. Serve immediately or chill until serving time.

5 TO 6 SERVINGS

ORANGE RICE PUDDING

This is a quick and delicious way to make rice pudding using leftover cooked rice.

    1 large orange
    1/3 cup sugar
    2 tablespoons cornstarch
    1 3/4 cups whole milk
    1 cup cooked rice

1. Grate the colored zest from the orange. Cut the orange in half and squeeze out 1/4 cup juice.

2. In a 2-quart saucepan, whisk together the sugar and cornstarch until well blended. Whisk in the milk until the mixture is thoroughly blended and the cornstarch is dissolved.

3. Cook over medium-high heat, whisking constantly, until the mixture boils and thickens, 4 to 6 minutes. Stir in the rice and boil, stirring, 1 minute. Remove from the heat.

4. Stir the orange zest and 1/4 cup juice into the pudding. Spoon into 5 or 6 dessert dishes. Cool 5 minutes. Serve warm or refrigerate until chilled.

5 TO 6 SERVINGS

JIFFY PEACHES AND CREAM MOUSSE

This creamy mousselike dessert is dotted throughout with chopped fresh peaches. It's also tasty made with chopped fresh nectarines or with berries: raspberries, blueberries or strawberries.

3 fresh peaches
1 cup heavy cream
1 package (8 ounces) cream cheese, softened
$\frac{1}{2}$ cup sugar
$\frac{1}{2}$ teaspoon vanilla or almond extract

1. Peel the peaches by submerging them in boiling water for 30 seconds, then rinsing with cold water and slipping off the skins. Coarsely chop the peaches, discarding the pits.

2. In a medium bowl with an electric mixer on high speed, beat the cream to stiff peaks. If you're using a stationary mixer, scrape the whipped cream into another bowl.

3. In the same mixer bowl with the same beaters (it's not necessary to wash either), beat the cream cheese with the sugar on medium speed until smooth. Beat in the vanilla until blended. With the mixer on low speed, gently beat in half of the whipped cream.

4. Remove the mixer and by hand, fold in the remaining whipped cream and the chopped peaches. Spoon the mousse into 6 stemmed dessert glasses or dishes, dividing evenly. Serve immediately or refrigerate until serving time.

6 SERVINGS

RASPBERRY WHIP

This last-minute dessert is simple to make and absolutely delicious. If you don't plan to serve it immediately, freeze for an hour or two. If frozen firm, the dessert may need to stand for a few minutes at room temperature to soften slightly before serving.

1 package (10 ounces) frozen raspberries in sugar syrup
1 cup heavy cream
2 teaspoons Grand Marnier or other orange liqueur
1 to 2 tablespoons powdered sugar

1. Thaw the berries in a microwave or in a bowl of warm water. Drain and reserve the syrup.

2. In a medium bowl with an electric beater on high speed, beat the cream to stiff peaks. With the mixer on low speed, quickly beat the drained raspberries into the whipped cream. Then fold in 1 tablespoon of the reserved raspberry syrup, the Grand Marnier and 1 tablespoon powdered sugar. Taste and add the remaining tablespoon sugar only if needed.

3. Spoon the berry whip into 4 stemmed glasses, dividing evenly. Serve immediately, garnished with shaved chocolate or fresh raspberries.

4 SERVINGS

STRAWBERRY WHIP

This light berry cream is ideal to serve over other berries, cut-up fresh fruit or slices of angel food cake.

4 ounces cream cheese, softened
1 cup sliced fresh strawberries
1/2 cup heavy cream
1/3 cup powdered sugar

1. In a medium bowl with an electric beater on medium-high speed, beat together the cream cheese and strawberries until as smooth as possible.

2. With the mixer on high speed, beat in the cream and powdered sugar until thickened like cream. Serve immediately or cover and refrigerate.

5 TO 6 SERVINGS

STRAWBERRY PINEAPPLE CLOUD

For variety, instead of strawberries try raspberries, blackberries, boysenberries or blueberries when they're in plentiful supply. Be sure to use sweetened pineapple as there is no added sugar in the recipe.

1 can (20 ounces) crushed pineapple packed in heavy syrup
2 pint baskets fresh strawberries
1 cup heavy cream
1 teaspoon vanilla extract
6 tablespoons shredded coconut, toasted if desired

1. Drain the pineapple well, pressing out as much excess syrup as possible. Discard the syrup or reserve for another use.

2. Rinse, drain and hull the strawberries. Reserve 6 of the nicest berries for garnish. Cut up the remaining berries and divide evenly among 6 stemmed dessert dishes or balloon wineglasses.

3. Meanwhile, in a medium bowl with an electric mixer on high speed, beat the cream with the vanilla to soft peaks. Fold the drained pineapple into the whipped cream.

4. Spoon the pineapple cream over the strawberries. Garnish each serving with 1 tablespoon coconut and a reserved whole strawberry. Serve immediately or cover and refrigerate until serving time.

6 SERVINGS

HOLIDAY EGGNOG TAPIOCA

When you have extra store-bought eggnog on hand at holiday time, this is a good way to use it up.

> 3 tablespoons quick-cooking tapioca
> 2½ cups commercial eggnog
> ¾ teaspoon vanilla or rum extract
> Sweetened whipped cream (from a pressurized can)
> Grated nutmeg

1. Place the tapioca in a 1½-quart microwave-safe glass bowl. Stir in the eggnog until well blended and let stand 3 to 4 minutes.

2. Microwave on High for 6 minutes, or until bubbly and thickened, stopping every 2 minutes to mix well. Remove from the microwave and stir in the vanilla.

3. Pour the pudding into 4 dessert dishes. Let stand for 5 to 10 minutes before serving warm, or refrigerate until chilled.

4. At serving time, garnish the top of each dessert with a pouf of whipped cream and dust with a dash of nutmeg.

4 SERVINGS

4 ESPECIALLY CHOCOLATE

Chocolate lovers rejoice! A glorious collection of quick desserts chock-full of your favorite flavor awaits you here. Among them are familiar classics and new creations that will make you want to run, not walk, into the kitchen. And, of course, all require only five ingredients and ten minutes or less of your busy time.

Selections range from a spectacular Chocolate Truffle Torte to dense, dark and, oh, so rich Mint Brownie Sundaes to simple but sophisticated Chocolate Pots de Crème and Chocolate Raspberry Trifle. For more homey options, try the yummy Chocolate Orange Fondue.

While most of the recipes are ready to serve immediately, a few, such as the sinfully rich Chocolate Silk Tart and the tasty Chocolate Angel Dessert, require a short time in the refrigerator to chill or set up.

The kind of chocolate you use is a matter of personal taste. Some like bittersweet, while others prefer semisweet or milk chocolate. Both domestic and imported chocolates are available for cooking and eating. While it's feasible to use imported European chocolate in these recipes, I found good-quality domestic brands yielded excellent results. In fact, as you'll notice, semisweet chocolate chips are called for in many of these recipes. They're a terrific time-saver because they require no cutting or chopping and melt quickly in the microwave. If you prefer, substitute bittersweet chocolate in any recipe calling for semisweet. But never attempt to substitute unsweetened baking chocolate for either semisweet or bittersweet chocolate, as it contains no sugar.

Store chocolate in a cool, dry place where the temperature ranges from 60 to 75 degrees F. At higher temperatures or fluctuating hot and cold temperatures, chocolate may acquire a pale-grayish-white dull bloom on the surface, which is caused by the cocoa butter melting and rising to the surface. Don't be alarmed; the bloom will not affect the flavor. It is safe to eat, and once melted, the chocolate will regain its original color.

The fastest way to melt chocolate and stay within the ten-minute time limit of this book is in the microwave oven, a method I highly recommend and have used for years. Heat the chocolate, uncovered, in a glass measuring cup, custard cup or bowl in the microwave on High for 1 to 2 minutes (depending on the amount), or according to the time specified in each recipe. Watch carefully and check often. The melted chocolate will appear still solid. When its appearance changes from dull to shiny, stir until smooth and melted. If necessary, return the chocolate to the microwave oven for a few seconds to melt any lumps.

Because of its delicate nature, white chocolate is best heated on Medium power in the microwave oven. And be sure any utensil you plan to use for melting chocolate is completely dry. Otherwise you run the risk of having the chocolate stiffen (or seize) up into a solid unusable lump.

When you want to splurge on some sin-sational chocolate dessert, simply turn the pages and read on. You're guaranteed to find a sweet to dream about.

FOOD PROCESSOR
CHOCOLATE MOUSSE

Make this silky smooth chocolate mousse with a food processor. Although the machine doesn't whip as much air into the cream as a beater on high speed, it works fine in this instance.

1 cup heavy cream
1 cup semisweet chocolate chips
1 egg
⅓ cup sugar
2 tablespoons coffee-flavored liqueur, such as Kahlúa

1. In a food processor, process the cream until stiff. Transfer to another bowl. Do not rinse out the food processor.

2. Place the chocolate chips and egg in the food processor. Mix until well blended.

3. In a glass measure or bowl, combine the sugar and ¼ cup of water. Microwave on High for 1 minute, or until boiling. Turn on the food processor and add the hot syrup through the feed tube. Process until the chocolate is melted. Add the coffee liqueur and process until mixed.

4. Transfer the mixture to a bowl. Cool by placing in the freezer for 5 minutes (no longer or mixture will become too firm).

5. Fold in the stiffly beaten cream until well blended. Divide the mousse among 4 dessert dishes. Cover and refrigerate 1 hour, or until set.

4 SERVINGS

CHEWY CHOCOLATE SQUARES

These are chewy and delicious. Dust with a little sifted powdered sugar before serving, if desired, for added appeal.

About 7 ounces chocolate wafer cookies (¾ of a 9-ounce box)
1 can (14 ounces) sweetened condensed milk
1 teaspoon vanilla extract
1 package (6 ounces) semisweet chocolate chips
1 cup chopped pecans or walnuts (4 ounces)

1. In a food processor or blender, grind the cookies into crumbs. There should be 1½ cups.

2. In a medium bowl, mix together the cookie crumbs, sweetened condensed milk and vanilla until well blended. Stir in the chocolate chips and chopped nuts.

3. Spread evenly in a generously buttered 6½-by-10-inch glass baking dish. Microwave on Medium for 6 minutes, turning the dish once. Microwave on High for 3 to 4 minutes, or until the mixture looks almost set (it will firm up as it cools, so do not overcook).

4. Let cool, then cut into squares.

MAKES ABOUT 28 COOKIES

CHOCOLATE SILK TART

1 refrigerated all-ready 9-inch pie crust
1 package (6 ounces) semisweet chocolate chips or 6 ounces
   bittersweet chocolate, cut up
6 tablespoons unsalted butter, at room temperature
⅓ cup powdered sugar
1 egg

1. Preheat the oven to 450 degrees F. Meanwhile, remove the pie crust from the refrigerator and let it stand at room temperature for 10 minutes.

2. Unfold the crust, remove the top plastic sheet and press out the fold lines. Place the crust in a 9½-inch fluted tart pan with a removable bottom. Remove the second plastic sheet and ease the crust into the pan, pressing firmly against the bottom and sides. Fold under the edge of the crust along the top edge of the pan so the crust is even with it. Pierce all over the bottom and sides with a fork. Bake the crust for 10 minutes, or until light golden. Let cool.

3. Meanwhile, place the chocolate in a small glass bowl. Microwave on High for 1½ to 2 minutes, or until smooth and melted when stirred; let cool a minute or two.

4. In a medium bowl, with an electric mixer on high speed, beat the butter and powdered sugar until light and fluffy. Beat in the egg until the mixture is fluffy and smooth. Beat in the melted chocolate until smooth and fluffy. Turn into the cool tart crust, spreading evenly. Refrigerate until chilled, at least 1 hour.

8 TO 10 SERVINGS

10-MINUTE BROWNIES

These are far superior to packaged brownies, and you can make them in less time than it takes to drive to the store and buy a mix. Although it is an extra ingredient, you can stir in ½ cup chopped nuts before microwaving the brownies, if you like.

8 tablespoons (1 stick) butter
2 squares (1 ounce each) unsweetened chocolate
1 cup sugar
2 eggs
½ cup flour

1. Place the butter in a 1½-quart glass bowl. Break up the unsweetened chocolate and add to the bowl. Microwave on High for 1½ to 2 minutes, or until the chocolate is melted and smooth when stirred.

2. With a fork, beat the sugar and eggs into the chocolate butter until well blended. Beat in the flour until thoroughly mixed. Spread evenly in a wax paper-lined 10-by-6-inch or 8-inch square glass dish.

3. Microwave on High for 3 minutes. Turn the dish a quarter turn and microwave for 2½ to 3 minutes longer. Avoid overcooking. Let cool, then cut into squares.

MAKES 16 BROWNIES

CHOCOLATE POTS DE CREME

These come together in a jiffy with the food processor and microwave, but they do require a couple of hours to set up in the refrigerator, so plan ahead.

³/₄ cup milk
1½ cups semisweet chocolate chips (9 ounces)
  3 tablespoons sugar
1½ tablespoons vegetable oil
1½ teaspoons vanilla extract

1. In a 2-cup glass measure, microwave the milk on High for about 2 minutes, until boiling.

2. Meanwhile, in a food processor, combine the chocolate chips, sugar, oil and vanilla. Turn on the machine and add the hot milk through the feed tube, processing until the mixture is smooth and well blended. Scrape down the sides of the bowl, if necessary.

3. Pour into 4 (³/₄-cup) dessert or custard cups or soufflé dishes. Cover and refrigerate until set, 1 to 2 hours.

4 SERVINGS

CHOCOLATE RASPBERRY POTS DE CRÈME: Stir 2 to 3 tablespoons fresh raspberries into the chocolate mixture in each dish before refrigerating.

QUICK CHOCOLATE MOUSSE

This rich dessert is made without any eggs. If you enjoy gourmet coffees, try the recipe with a flavored brew, such as chocolate raspberry or hazelnut.

1 cup semisweet chocolate chips (6 ounces)
1/3 cup strong freshly brewed coffee
1 teaspoon vanilla extract
1 cup heavy cream

1. In a 2-cup glass measure, combine the chocolate chips and coffee. Microwave on High for 1 minute, or until the chocolate is melted and the mixture is smooth when stirred. Stir in the vanilla.

2. To cool quickly, place over a bowl of ice water filled with ice cubes and stir often (do not allow the mixture to get thick and lumpy).

3. Meanwhile, in a medium bowl with an electric mixer on high speed, beat the cream to stiff peaks. Fold the cooled chocolate into half of the whipped cream until blended. Fold in the remaining whipped cream.

4. Spoon the mousse into 4 stemmed glasses or dessert dishes, dividing evenly. Serve immediately or refrigerate 1 to 2 hours or until serving time.

4 SERVINGS

CHOCOLATE TRUFFLE TORTE

This decadent creation is spectacular and always garners raves. It's creamy and smooth and tastes like a big chocolate truffle. Be sure to serve small slices, as this dessert is exceptionally rich.

12 to 14 pecan shortbread cookies
1 pound bittersweet or semisweet chocolate
2 1/2 cups heavy cream
1 1/2 cups chopped pecans (6 ounces)
1 jar (about 12 ounces) caramel sauce

1. In a food processor, grind enough cookies to make 1 1/2 cups crumbs. Coarsely chop the chocolate.

2. Line an 8- or 8 1/2-inch springform pan with the cookie crumbs, pressing them over the bottom and about 3/4 inch up the sides of the pan.

3. In a 2-quart glass bowl, combine the chocolate and 1 1/2 cups of the cream. Microwave on High for 1 1/2 minutes; stir well. Microwave for 30 to 45 seconds longer, until the chocolate is melted and the mixture is smooth when stirred.

4. Mix in the chopped pecans. Scrape the chocolate mixture into the crumb-lined pan, spreading carefully and evenly. Cover and refrigerate 2 to 3 hours, or until firm.

5. To serve, warm the caramel sauce in a microwave oven. Whip the remaining 1 cup cream. Cut thin slices and top with the whipped cream. Pass the warm caramel sauce on the side.

12 SERVINGS

CHOCOLATE-COATED FRUIT

1 dozen large to medium-large fresh strawberries
1 ripe kiwifruit
1 cup semisweet chocolate chips (6 ounces)
1 tablespoon vegetable oil or solid vegetable shortening
8 dried peaches

1. Rinse the strawberries and dry well on paper towels; do not hull. Peel the kiwifruit and cut crosswise into 5 or 6 slices. Drain any excess liquid from the fruit on paper towels.

2. In a 2-cup glass measure, combine the chocolate chips and the oil. Microwave on Medium for 2 minutes; stir well. Microwave on Medium for 1 to 1½ minutes longer, or just until the chocolate is melted and smooth when stirred. Do not overheat.

3. Holding onto the green stem of the strawberries, dip one at a time into the chocolate, coating about three-quarters of the berry (leave some of the red berry and green hull showing). Place the berries ¾ inch apart on a wax paper-lined jelly-roll pan.

4. Dip the peaches, one at a time, into the chocolate, coating about half of each one. Place on the same pan. Dip the kiwifruit, one slice at a time, into the chocolate, coating about half of the slice. Place on the jelly-roll pan.

5. Refrigerate until serving time or the chocolate sets, about 10 to 15 minutes. To serve, arrange the fruits attractively on a doily-lined platter and pass immediately.

6 TO 8 SERVINGS

CHOCOLATE RASPBERRY TRIFLE

1 package (3.4 ounces) instant vanilla pudding and pie filling
  mix
¾ cup milk
1 cup heavy cream
1 prepared chocolate loaf cake (15 ounces)
2 cups fresh raspberries

1. In a medium bowl, combine the pudding mix with the milk. Whisk 1½ to 2 minutes, or until well blended; the pudding will thicken as it is mixed.

2. In a medium bowl with an electric mixer on high speed, beat the cream to stiff peaks. Fold the whipped cream into the pudding until well blended.

3. Cut the loaf cake crosswise into ½-inch-thick slices.

4. To assemble the trifle, in a 2-quart glass serving bowl, arrange 4 or 5 of the pound cake slices to cover the bottom of the dish and curve up the sides of the bowl. Spread half of the pudding mixture over the cake. Distribute 1 cup of the raspberries evenly over the pudding. Repeat these layers, using the remaining cake slices, pudding mixture and raspberries. Serve immediately or cover and refrigerate until serving time.

8 TO 10 SERVINGS

CHOCOLATE STRAWBERRY TRIFLE: Substitute 2 cups sliced strawberries for the raspberries called for above.

PEANUT BUTTER CUP TRUFFLE PIE

For those who love peanut butter cup candies and chocolate, this is sure to be a winner.

½ of a 15-ounce chocolate loaf cake
¾ cup heavy cream
3 cups semisweet chocolate chips (18 ounces)
3 packages (1.6 ounces each) peanut butter cups (6 cups total)
½ cup chopped peanuts (optional)

1. Cut the ½ loaf cake into ½-inch slices. Use the cake slices to line the bottom of a 9-inch pie pan, cutting as necessary so the bottom of the pan is completely covered and there are no spaces showing.

2. In a 1½-quart glass bowl, microwave the cream on High for 1 to 1½ minutes, until hot and bubbling. Add the chocolate and stir until melted and smooth. Cool 2 to 3 minutes.

3. Meanwhile, chop the peanut butter cups into ¾-inch pieces. Stir the chopped candy into the chocolate cream. Carefully pour this mixture over the cake lining the pie pan, spreading evenly.

4. Sprinkle the peanuts over the top. Refrigerate until the chocolate is set, 1 to 2 hours, or until serving time. To serve, cut into thin slices.

8 TO 10 SERVINGS

Chocolate Nut Ice Cream Balls

These are an easy home version of the Italian restaurant ice cream dessert known as *tartufo*.

1/2 cup chopped toasted pecans
3/4 cup chopped milk chocolate pieces (from a chocolate bar)
 4 large scoops vanilla, chocolate or coffee ice cream
3/4 cup prepared hot fudge sauce
3/4 teaspoon instant espresso powder

1. In a shallow bowl, toss together the pecans and the chocolate pieces.

2. Drop a scoop of ice cream into the nut-chocolate mixture and roll quickly to coat completely, pressing the mixture into the ice cream with your fingertips. Repeat with the remaining ice cream. As you finish each ball, set it in a dish or wrap in a piece of plastic wrap and place in the freezer.

3. In a small glass bowl, whisk together the fudge sauce and espresso powder until thoroughly blended. Microwave on High for 45 to 60 seconds, or until the sauce is warm when stirred.

4. To serve, spoon some of the warm fudge sauce over each of 4 dessert plates or in the bottom of 4 dessert bowls. Place an ice cream ball in the center of the sauce on each plate. Serve immediately.

4 SERVINGS

JIFFY CHOCOLATE PIE

Here's a dessert that's light, lovely and made in a flash.

  1 package (12 ounces) semisweet chocolate chips
  $\frac{1}{2}$ cup milk
  2 cups miniature marshmallows
  1$\frac{1}{2}$ cups heavy cream
  1 prepared 8-inch chocolate crumb crust

1. In a 1-quart glass bowl, combine the chocolate chips, milk and marshmallows. Microwave on High for 1 minute; stir. Microwave on High for 30 seconds, or until the marshmallows melt (don't heat any more than necessary because additional cooling time will be necessary). Cool 5 minutes.

2. Meanwhile, in a medium bowl with an electric mixer on high speed, beat the cream to soft peaks. Remove 1 cup of the whipped cream from the bowl and reserve.

3. Add half of the whipped cream remaining in the bowl to the cooled chocolate mixture and blend well. Fold in the remaining whipped cream from the bowl until thoroughly mixed.

4. Turn the chocolate mixture into the prepared crust, spreading evenly. Refrigerate 5 minutes.

5. Spread the reserved 1 cup whipped cream evenly over the top of the pie. Refrigerate 1 hour or longer, until serving time.

8 SERVINGS

CHOCOLATE ORANGE FONDUE

Bring back fondue for a quick dessert that's fun to eat. Serve each diner their own little ramekin of dipping chocolate (I use small soufflé cups) on an individual dessert plate and arrange a selection of cut-up fruits and squares of cake alongside.

2 dark mildly sweet chocolate bars, such as Hershey's (7 ounces each), or 14 ounces semisweet or bittersweet chocolate
1/2 cup heavy cream
1/4 cup orange juice
2 tablespoons Grand Marnier or other orange liqueur
Assorted dippers: seedless green grapes, whole strawberries, peeled peach slices, peeled orange segments, pound cake or angel food cake squares, large marshmallows, etc.

1. Break or cut the chocolate into pieces and place in a medium glass bowl. Add the cream and the orange juice. Microwave on High for 1½ minutes; stir. Microwave for about 1 minute longer, or until the chocolate is melted and the mixture is smooth when stirred and warm throughout. Stir in the Grand Marnier.

2. Transfer the chocolate to 6 or 8 individual ramekins, such as small soufflé dishes, and place on dessert plates.

3. Arrange an assortment of fruits, cake and marshmallows alongside to use for dipping into the chocolate with forks.

6 TO 8 SERVINGS; ABOUT 2 CUPS SAUCE

WINTER FRUITS WITH PORT CHOCOLATE SAUCE

Port wine and chocolate are a dynamic duo. Here they team in a chocolate sauce that is the ideal accompaniment for dried and fresh fruits.

1 cup chopped semisweet or bittersweet chocolate (6 ounces)
1/4 cup ruby port wine
3 bananas
24 dried apricot halves
3 ripe firm Bosc or other pears

1. In a 2-cup glass measure, combine the chocolate and port. Microwave on High for 1 to 1 1/4 minutes, or until the chocolate is melted and smooth when stirred. Stir in 1 tablespoon hot water, if desired, for a thinner sauce.

2. Peel the bananas. Cut half of each of the bananas into slices and place them on each of 6 dessert plates. Arrange 4 of the apricot halves around the edges of each plate.

3. Cut the unpeeled pears lengthwise in half. Scoop out the cores. Cut each pear half into lengthwise slices and arrange in the center of each of the dessert plates.

4. Drizzle the warm chocolate sauce over the fruit, dividing evenly among the 6 plates.

6 SERVINGS

FRUIT SKEWERS WITH MILK CHOCOLATE SAUCE

This is a fanciful, festive way to present dessert. Prepare the skewers ahead, store them in the refrigerator and pop them out at dessert time.

 8 ounces milk chocolate
1/2 cup heavy cream or milk
24 fresh strawberries (1 to 1 1/2 pint baskets)
 2 bananas
 1 small papaya

1. Cut the chocolate into chunks. In a small glass bowl or 2-cup glass measure, combine the chocolate and cream. Microwave on high for 1 minute; stir. Microwave for 30 to 60 seconds longer, or until the chocolate is melted and smooth when stirred. Set aside.

2. Rinse the strawberries and remove the green stems. Dry on paper towels. Peel the bananas and cut each into 8 slices. Peel the papaya and cut into 16 chunks about 1 by 1 1/2 inches.

3. On each of 8 bamboo or small stainless steel skewers, alternate 1 whole strawberry, a banana slice and a piece of papaya; repeat, ending with a berry.

4. Spoon 2 tablespoons of the chocolate sauce onto each of 4 dessert plates; tilt the plate to coat the bottom evenly. Arrange 2 fruit skewers on top of the chocolate sauce in the center of each plate. Drizzle 1 tablespoon of the remaining chocolate sauce over each and serve.

4 SERVINGS

CHOCOLATE ANGEL DESSERT

This is an updated variation on the angel dessert theme that was popular years ago. It's a tasty way to embellish angel food cake.

8 ounces angel food cake
1 cup semisweet chocolate chips (6 ounces)
1/4 cup strong freshly brewed coffee
3/4 cup heavy cream
1/2 cup milk chocolate English toffee chips (such as Heath Bits)

1. Cut the cake into 1-inch cubes. There should be about 5 cups.

2. In 2-cup glass measure, combine the chocolate chips and the coffee. Microwave on High for 50 to 60 seconds, until the chocolate is melted and smooth when stirred. Microwave only enough to melt the chocolate; avoid getting the mixture too hot so it won't melt the cream when it is mixed in. Transfer to a large bowl and cool 5 minutes.

3. In a medium bowl with an electric mixer on high speed, beat the cream to stiff peaks. Fold half of the whipped cream into the somewhat cooled chocolate mixture until well blended. Fold in the remaining whipped cream. Fold the cake cubes into the chocolate mixture until thoroughly coated.

4. Turn the mixture into a buttered 8-inch springform pan, spreading evenly. Sprinkle the toffee chips evenly over the top. Cover and refrigerate for 30 minutes, or longer until serving. To serve, remove the side of the springform pan and cut into slices.

6 TO 7 SERVINGS

MINT BROWNIE SUNDAES

The combination of mint and chocolate is unbeatable as this sundae proves. Use your favorite store-bought or bakery brownies.

1 package (10 ounces) mint semisweet chocolate chips
½ cup milk
6 brownies, about 3 inches square
1½ pints chocolate or vanilla ice cream
Sweetened whipped cream (optional)

1. In a 1-quart glass bowl, combine the mint chocolate chips and the milk. Microwave on High for 1 minute; stir well. Microwave for 30 to 45 seconds longer, until the chocolate is melted and the mixture is smooth when stirred.

2. Place 1 brownie on each of 6 dessert plates or shallow bowls. Top with a large scoop of ice cream.

3. Drizzle the mint sauce over all. Top with a dollop of whipped cream, if desired. Serve immediately.

6 SERVINGS

MILK CHOCOLATE BROWNIE BANANA SUNDAES

Kids adore this combination. A slice of unfrosted chocolate cake can be used for the base in place of the brownie. And feel free to choose your favorite flavor ice cream.

1 package (11.5 ounces) milk chocolate chips
⅓ cup milk
3 bananas
6 unfrosted brownies
6 scoops chocolate or vanilla ice cream

1. In a small glass bowl, combine the chocolate chips and the milk. Microwave on High for 1 to 1½ minutes, or until the chocolate is melted and smooth when stirred.

2. Peel and slice the bananas.

3. Place a brownie in each of 6 serving bowls. Top with a scoop of ice cream. Arrange the banana slices around the ice cream and spoon the chocolate sauce on top. Serve immediately.

6 SERVINGS

EASIEST-EVER MICROWAVE CHOCOLATE SAUCE

When you need chocolate sauce fast, whip this one up. It's a favorite standby at our house and not only tastes better than store-bought, it is more economical, too. To vary the flavor, add a tablespoon of Grand Marnier, brandy, crème de menthe or other favorite liqueur or a small amount of almond or rum extract. This recipe doubles easily. To do so, simply increase the microwave time by 30 to 60 seconds.

1 cup semisweet chocolate chips (6 ounces)
1/4 cup milk or heavy cream
1/4 teaspoon vanilla extract

1. In a 2-cup glass measure, combine the chocolate chips and the milk. Microwave on High for 45 to 60 seconds; stir until the chocolate is melted and the mixture is smooth. If necessary, return to microwave for 15 to 20 seconds. Stir in the vanilla.

2. Serve immediately over ice cream, sorbet or cake slices or use to make banana splits. Keep any leftovers refrigerated and reheat in the microwave before serving.

MAKES ABOUT 3/4 CUP SAUCE

5 WARM DESSERTS

Fragrant, warm desserts are particularly welcome in the colder months or after a light meal. Fruits in season often take well to light cooking, and they offer tremendous variety of flavor along with attractive jewel-like colors. Some of these desserts include Stir-Fried Glazed Plums, Raspberry-Sauced Blintzes with Sour Cream, Warm Fruit Salad, Pineapple Fritters, Creamy Raspberry Broil; there are many more.

The broiler, conventional oven, microwave and stove top are used to make these warm goodies. It might surprise you that the conventional oven is on the equipment list, but in a jiffy you can bake up recipes like Fruit and Nut Turnovers with packaged filo dough. Many fruits, such as raspberries, peaches, nectarines and apples, do beautifully under the broiler.

Other finales to savor include Caramel Apple Slices, made with apple slices, bottled caramel flavor topping, cinnamon and chopped pecans; Bananas in Rum Cream Sauce and Pineapple Fritters, whipped up in a flash using buttermilk pancake mix. For a quick, single-ingredient sauce, melt vanilla ice cream and spoon it over all.

Apple Crisp, with its cinnamon-oatmeal topping, and Microwave Peach Cobbler with Buttermilk Biscuit Topping are great *5 in 10* adaptations of the American classics. Both are fine on their own or topped with a scoop of ice cream or a dollop of whipped cream.

APPLE CRISP

Use a microwave oven and the broiler to make this old-fashioned dessert in a hurry. Top with vanilla ice cream or whipped cream.

6 medium Granny Smith apples
³/₄ cup packed brown sugar
¹/₂ cup quick-cooking rolled oats
³/₄ teaspoon ground cinnamon
4 tablespoons butter

1. Peel, core and slice the apples. Place in a 9-inch glass pie dish. Cover with wax paper. Microwave on High for about 6 minutes, turning the dish as necessary, until the apples are tender.

2. Meanwhile, preheat the oven broiler. In a small bowl, combine the brown sugar, oatmeal and cinnamon. Mix well. With 2 knives or a pastry blender, cut in the butter until the mixture is crumbly.

3. Sprinkle the crumbly mixture evenly over the apples. Broil about 6 inches from the heat 2¹/₂ to 3 minutes, or until the top is bubbly and browned. Let stand a couple of minutes, then spoon into serving dishes and serve warm.

4 TO 5 SERVINGS

CARAMEL APPLE SLICES

Rely on bottled caramel topping mixed with a little cinnamon for this tasty apple dessert that goes together in a flash in the microwave.

4 tart-sweet cooking apples
1/2 cup bottled caramel flavor topping
1/2 teaspoon ground cinnamon
1/2 cup chopped pecans
    Sweetened whipped cream (from a pressurized can) or
    coffee or butter pecan ice cream

1. Core the apples and peel, if desired. Cut the apples into 3/8-inch slices. Arrange the slices in a 9-inch glass pie dish.

2. In a small bowl, mix together the caramel topping and ground cinnamon until blended. Drizzle over the apples. Sprinkle the pecans on top.

3. Cover the dish with microwave-safe plastic wrap. Microwave on High for 6 to 7 minutes, or until the apples are fork-tender. Check and turn once during cooking.

4. Serve immediately topped with the whipped cream or spoon the apple-caramel mixture over scoops of ice cream.

4 TO 6 SERVINGS

CINNAMONY GLAZED APPLE SLICES

A sensational easy dessert that provides a wonderful way to enjoy apples. Serve topped with whipped cream or ice cream.

  4 large tart green apples
  ²/₃ cup sugar
1¹/₂ teaspoons ground cinnamon
  6 tablespoons unsalted butter
    Whipped cream or vanilla ice cream

1. Peel and core the apples and cut them into ¹/₄-inch slices. In a medium bowl, toss the apples with the sugar and cinnamon, mixing well to coat the apples.

2. In a large (12-inch) frying pan, melt the butter over medium heat. Add the apple slices and raise the heat to medium-high. Cover and cook for 2 minutes. Uncover and cook, stirring occasionally with a wooden spoon, until lightly browned, 3 to 4 minutes longer.

3. Divide the apples and sauce evenly among 4 dessert plates. Serve topped with whipped cream or a scoop of ice cream.

4 SERVINGS

MICROWAVE MAPLE BAKED APPLES

Served right out of the microwave or refrigerated until cold, these are terrific.

2 large baking apples, preferably Rome Beauty
1 tablespoon brown sugar
1/4 teaspoon ground cinnamon
1 tablespoon raisins
2 tablespoons maple syrup

1. Peel around the top of the apples to about halfway down; leave the skin on the bottom half. Core the apples, being careful not to cut through the bottoms. Stand the apples up in a medium heatproof glass casserole dish.

2. In a small bowl, mix together the brown sugar, cinnamon and raisins. Stuff the cored apples with this mixture. Drizzle the maple syrup into the center of the apples and all over them. Cover the dish with microwave-safe plastic wrap and pierce the top in several places.

3. Microwave on High for 4 to 5 minutes, turning the dish twice, until the apples are tender. Let stand, covered, 2 to 3 minutes. Serve warm or refrigerate until serving time.

2 SERVINGS

QUICK BANANAS FOSTER STYLE

Based on the classic New Orleans specialty, this version is quick and contains only 5 ingredients. Traditionally the bananas and syrup are spooned over vanilla ice cream.

2 bananas
2 tablespoons butter
2 tablespoons brown sugar
1/4 cup dark or amber rum
1/8 teaspoon ground cinnamon

1. Peel the bananas. Cut them in half lengthwise, then in half horizontally.

2. In a medium frying pan, cook the butter and brown sugar over medium heat, stirring, until the sugar dissolves, 1 to 2 minutes. Add the rum and cinnamon.

3. Add the bananas to the skillet and continue to cook over medium heat 2 to 3 minutes, turning to coat the bananas with the syrup, until they are slightly softened but not mushy.

2 SERVINGS

BANANAS IN RUM CREAM SAUCE

Try this easy skillet dessert from my friend Susan Wyler on its own or over vanilla ice cream.

4 bananas
3 tablespoons unsalted butter
1/3 cup packed dark brown sugar
3 tablespoons dark rum
1 cup heavy cream

1. Peel the bananas and cut in half lengthwise, then crosswise so you end up with 4 pieces each.

2. In a large skillet, melt the butter over medium heat. Add the banana pieces to the pan and cook, turning once or twice, until the bananas are lightly browned but still firm and not mushy, about 1 to 2 minutes. Remove the bananas to a plate.

3. Add the brown sugar to the pan and cook, stirring, until caramelized and bubbly, about 1 minute. Add the rum and cook, stirring, 15 seconds. Pour in the cream and boil over high heat, stirring constantly, until the sauce is slightly thickened, 1½ to 2 minutes.

4. Arrange the bananas on 4 serving plates. Spoon the sauce over all, dividing evenly. Serve immediately.

4 SERVINGS

BROILED NECTARINES

This is a lovely way to eat fresh nectarines. If amaretti cookies are hard to come by, substitute soft macaroons, pecan sandies or even vanilla wafer cookies. Peaches are also good prepared this way.

4 ripe nectarines
2 teaspoons lemon juice
3 tablespoons light brown sugar
$1/4$ teaspoon grated nutmeg
$1/2$ cup amaretti cookie crumbs (about 8 cookies)

1. Cut the nectarines into $1/4$-inch-thick slices and place in a medium bowl. Add the lemon juice, brown sugar and nutmeg and toss until well mixed. Divide the nectarines evenly among 4 ($5^{1}/2$-inch) round shallow ovenproof ramekins.

2. Preheat the oven broiler. Broil the nectarines 6 inches from the heat source for about 5 minutes, or until bubbly around the edges.

3. Sprinkle the cookie crumbs over the top of the fruit, dividing evenly. Broil for 1 to $1^{1}/2$ minutes longer, or until the crumbs are very lightly browned. Serve warm.

4 SERVINGS

NECTARINE CUSTARD CAKE BROIL

The idea for this evolved from a much more complex dessert sampled at a restaurant in a San Francisco hotel. This dessert looks pretty, tastes great and, unlike the original version, goes together easily with convenience products.

3 nectarines
½ package (3.4 ounces) instant vanilla pudding and pie filling mix
1⅓ cups milk
6 slices of chocolate loaf or all-butter pound cake, cut ½ inch thick
6 tablespoons sliced almonds

1. Preheat the oven broiler. Cut the nectarines into ¼-inch slices.

2. In a medium bowl, whisk together the pudding mix and milk for 1 to 2 minutes, until smooth and slightly thickened.

3. Place a slice of the cake in each of 6 (5½-inch) round ovenproof ramekins or individual gratin dishes. Arrange a row of nectarine slices down the center of each cake slice. Spoon a generous ¼ cup vanilla sauce over the nectarines and cake in each ramekin. Sprinkle 1 tablespoon of the almonds over the top of each dessert.

4. Broil 6 inches from the heat for 2½ to 3 minutes, or until the almonds are lightly browned.

6 SERVINGS

SAUTEED NECTARINES

A wonderful, simple way to enjoy the bounty of summer fruits. Another time, try fresh peaches or plums.

2 large firm ripe nectarines
2 tablespoons butter
3 tablespoons light brown sugar
2 tablespoons heavy cream
1 tablespoon bourbon

1. Cut the nectarines into slices; discard the pits.

2. Melt the butter in a medium frying pan over medium heat until hot. Stir in the brown sugar and cook, stirring, until the mixture bubbles. Add the cream and cook, stirring, until thickened and smooth, 1 to 2 minutes.

3. Stir the bourbon into the pan and add the nectarine slices. Cook, stirring often, until they are heated through and coated with the sauce, 1 to 2 minutes. Spoon onto 2 dessert plates.

2 SERVINGS

STIR-FRIED GLAZED PLUMS

When ripe plums are in season, this is an appealing way to cook them up in a jiffy.

6 large black plums
1/4 cup packed light brown sugar
1 tablespoon lemon juice
1/4 cup heavy cream
1/4 cup sliced almonds

1. Cut the unpeeled plums into slices and discard the pits.

2. In a large frying pan, combine the plums, brown sugar and lemon juice. Heat to boiling over high heat, stirring occasionally.

3. Reduce the heat to medium-high and cook, stirring occasionally, until the plums are tender but not mushy, 3 to 4 minutes. Stir in the cream and cook 1 minute longer.

4. Spoon onto 4 dessert plates and top each serving with 1 tablespoon almonds. Serve immediately.

4 SERVINGS

STIR-FRIED CINNAMON-GLAZED PLUMS: In step 3, instead of the heavy cream, stir in 1/2 teaspoon ground cinnamon.

BROILED PINEAPPLE SLICES

For a comforting fresh fruit dessert, try these warm, fragrant pineapple slices. They're good by themselves or topped with vanilla or butter pecan ice cream.

1 large pineapple
2 tablespoons butter
6 tablespoons brown sugar
$1/2$ teaspoon ground cinnamon

1. Peel the pineapple. Core it and slice crosswise into $1/2$-inch rings. Place the slices on a 10-by-15-inch jelly-roll pan.

2. Preheat the oven broiler. Meanwhile, in a small glass bowl, microwave the butter on High for 30 to 45 seconds, until melted. Stir in the brown sugar and cinnamon. Spread the mixture evenly over the pineapple slices.

3. Broil 6 to 7 inches from the heat for 3 to 5 minutes, or until lightly caramelized and bubbly. Watch carefully to be sure the topping doesn't burn. Serve hot or warm, with a knife and fork.

4 TO 6 SERVINGS

PINEAPPLE FRITTERS

Be sure to serve these hot, sprinkled with powdered sugar. If pineapple doesn't suit your fancy, the fritters are delicious prepared with five or six bananas peeled and halved in both directions.

1 can (20 ounces) pineapple slices packed in juice
1/2 cup canola oil
2/3 cup buttermilk pancake mix
3 tablespoons powdered sugar
   Sweetened whipped cream (from a pressurized can)

1. Drain the pineapple. Heat the oil in a large frying pan over medium-high heat until hot.

2. Place the pancake mix in a shallow bowl. Coat both sides of the pineapple slices, one at a time, with the dry pancake mix, shaking off any excess.

3. Fry the pineapple slices in the hot oil in 2 or 3 batches without crowding, turning once, until golden brown, 1 1/2 to 2 minutes total. With a slotted spoon, remove to a double thickness of paper towels to drain.

4. Transfer the fritters to dessert plates. Sift the powdered sugar over the top of the pineapple fritters. Serve hot, topped with whipped cream, if desired.

4 TO 5 SERVINGS

PLUMS POACHED IN RED WINE

These plums with a dash of red wine are beautiful looking and wonderful tasting.

4 large black plums
$1/3$ cup sugar
1 teaspoon vanilla extract
$1/4$ cup dry red wine

1. Cut the plums in half; remove and discard the pits. Cut the plums into $3/8$-inch slices; there should be about 3 cups.

2. In a medium glass bowl, combine the plums, sugar and vanilla. Mix well. Cover with microwave-safe plastic wrap. Microwave on High for 4 to 5 minutes, turning the dish once, until the plums are almost soft.

3. Stir in the red wine. Spoon some of the plums and their juices into each of 4 dessert dishes, dividing evenly. Serve warm, at room temperature or chilled.

4 SERVINGS

CREAMY RASPBERRY BROIL

This is easy and surprisingly tasty. Try the same technique with fresh peaches, fresh strawberries or almost any in-season fruit.

1 package (12 ounces) frozen unsweetened raspberries (do
   not thaw) or 3 cups fresh raspberries or strawberries
$^2/_3$ cup sour cream
$^1/_2$ cup light brown sugar

1. Preheat the oven broiler. If using fresh berries, rinse them well and drain in a colander. Pat dry on paper towels.

2. Divide the raspberries evenly among 4 individual ($5^3/_4$-inch) round ovenproof baking or gratin dishes.

3. Spoon 2 generous tablespoons of sour cream into each dish of raspberries and spread evenly to almost cover the fruit. Sprinkle 2 tablespoons of the brown sugar over each serving.

4. Broil 6 inches from the heat for $1^1/_2$ to 2 minutes, watching carefully, until most of the brown sugar is melted. Serve immediately.

4 SERVINGS

RASPBERRY-SAUCED BLINTZES WITH SOUR CREAM

If you like blintzes, try this dressed-up version. Use frozen berries to make the warm sauce.

1 package (13 ounces) frozen cheese blintzes
2 tablespoons unsalted butter
2 cups frozen raspberries or frozen assorted berries, partially thawed
2 tablespoons apricot preserves
6 tablespoons sour cream

1. If necessary, thaw the blintzes in a microwave oven.

2. In a large frying pan, melt the butter over medium-high heat. Add the blintzes, seam-sides up, and cook over medium-high heat until golden brown, watching carefully, about 2 to 3 minutes. Turn over and continue cooking over medium to medium-high heat 2 to 3 minutes longer, or until light golden. Remove to a plate and keep warm.

3. To make the raspberry sauce, in a medium nonreactive frying pan, heat the raspberries with the apricot preserves over medium heat until warm or hot, stirring occasionally. Be careful not to break up all of the berries (some should be left whole).

4. Place 1 or 2 blintzes on each dessert plate. Top with some of the raspberry sauce, dividing evenly among the plates. Top with a dollop of the sour cream. Serve immediately.

3 TO 6 SERVINGS

STRAWBERRIES IN RUM SAUCE

1 pint basket fresh strawberries
1 tablespoon butter
$\frac{1}{3}$ cup packed light brown sugar
$\frac{1}{4}$ cup rum
4 slices of pound cake or 1 pint vanilla ice cream

1. Rinse, dry, hull and slice the strawberries.

2. In a large frying pan, melt the butter over medium heat. Stir in the brown sugar and rum and heat to boiling. Boil over medium-high heat, stirring once or twice, until the sauce has thickened just slightly, 2 or 3 minutes.

3. Stir in the strawberries and remove from the heat. Immediately serve some of the berries and sauce spooned over the pound cake slices or scoops of vanilla ice cream.

4 SERVINGS

WARM FRUIT SALAD

Serve this tempting mélange on top of cake slices or ice cream for a fragrant cinnamon-scented winter dessert. It makes a wonderful finale to a homey meal.

⅓ cup packed brown sugar
1½ teaspoons ground cinnamon
  1 can (29 ounces) sliced cling peaches in heavy syrup
  1 can (20 ounces) pineapple chunks packed in unsweetened juice
  1 can (16 ounces) fruit cocktail in extra light syrup

1. In a 1½- to 2-quart glass bowl or casserole dish, mix together the brown sugar and cinnamon.

2. Drain the fruits, discarding the juices. Mix the fruits gently into the brown sugar mixture until well blended.

3. Cover the dish with microwave-safe plastic wrap. Microwave on High for 6 minutes, stirring once. Remove the plastic wrap. Microwave on High, uncovered, for 2 to 3 minutes, or until hot throughout.

4. Spoon some of the fruits with the juices in the bowl into dessert dishes. Serve hot, warm or at room temperature.

4 TO 6 SERVINGS

MICROWAVE PEACH COBBLER WITH BUTTERMILK BISCUIT TOPPING

Ready-to-bake refrigerated buttermilk biscuits top this quick and easy cobbler.

1/3 cup plus 1 tablespoon sugar
 1 tablespoon cornstarch
 2 bags (16 ounces each) thawed frozen peach slices
 1 container (5 ounces) refrigerated buttermilk biscuits
1/2 teaspoon ground cinnamon

1. In a small bowl, mix together 1/3 cup of the sugar and the cornstarch until thoroughly blended. In a deep-dish 9-inch glass pie plate or 10-inch regular glass pie plate, toss the fruit with the sugar and cornstarch until all of the fruit is well coated.

2. Microwave on High for 6 to 7 minutes, stirring every 3 minutes, until the juices start to clear and thicken.

3. Split each biscuit crosswise into 2 thinner biscuits. Arrange the biscuits over the top of the peaches. In a small bowl, stir together the remaining 1 tablespoon sugar and the cinnamon until well mixed. Sprinkle the cinnamon sugar over the tops of the biscuits.

4. Microwave on High for 3 to 4 minutes, or until the biscuits are cooked through. Let stand for 5 minutes before serving.

4 TO 5 SERVINGS

FRUIT AND NUT TURNOVERS

1/2 cup chopped mixed dried fruits (dried apricots and prunes
   are a good combination)
1/2 cup chopped almonds or walnuts
 2 tablespoons apricot-pineapple or other flavor preserves
 4 tablespoons unsalted butter
 4 filo dough sheets, each about 13 by 17 inches

1. Preheat the oven to 375 degrees F. In a small bowl, mix together the dried fruits, nuts and preserves. Place the butter in a small glass bowl. Microwave on High 40 to 45 seconds, or until melted.

2. Unwrap the filo dough sheets and place on a large sheet of waxed paper. Cover with wax paper and a damp towel. Remove 1 filo dough sheet to another large sheet of wax paper; brush with some of the melted butter. Top with a second filo sheet and brush with more butter. Top with a third and fourth filo sheet, brushing each layer with butter.

3. With a sharp knife, cut the filo into 12 squares, each about 4 inches. Place some of the fruit mixture in one corner of each square, dividing the mixture evenly. Brush the edges with the remaining butter and fold over the other half of the dough to cover the fruit mixture and form a triangle. Press the edges together firmly with your fingers to seal. Place the triangles on an ungreased baking sheet.

4. Bake about 10 minutes, or until the filo is a rich golden brown. Serve warm or at room temperature.

MAKES 12 TURNOVERS

6 COOL FRUITS

It's amazing what a dazzling and versatile array of fruit desserts you can whip up in ten minutes or less with only five ingredients. Selections range from simple Raspberries with Quick Crème Fraîche and Pineapple with Kirsch to trendy Strawberries in Balsamic Vinegar (don't make a face until you try it!) and Tropical Fruit Salad with Toasted Coconut. There is also a variation on the melba theme with raspberries and pineapple.

Although the emphasis in these recipes is on using in-season fresh fruits, you'll find that some specifically call for frozen, dried or canned fruits. While substitutes are feasible within like kinds of fruits (fresh raspberries for fresh strawberries, for example), for best results, don't attempt to use fresh, frozen, dried or canned fruits interchangeably unless the tested recipe specifically recommends doing so.

Be sure to use the highest quality ripe but firm fresh fruit. And for best flavor, make a recipe while the fruit is at its peak and a good buy. Avoid using imported fruits that are out of season. Not only are they extremely expensive, but more often than not they lack flavor, juiciness and texture.

In the winter, opt for desserts based on apples, bananas, pears or oranges or those featuring canned, dried or frozen fruits. Spring and summer offer the largest variety of choices, ranging from strawberries and raspberries to blueberries, melons, peaches, plums, nectarines and much more.

FRUIT AMBROSIA

Refreshing and a cinch to toss together.

1 can (15 ounces) mandarin oranges
1 can (20 ounces) pineapple chunks packed in juice
1 cup lightly packed shredded sweetened coconut
1 cup sour cream
  Sliced toasted almonds or maraschino cherries, for garnish

1. Drain the mandarin oranges and pineapple chunks well.

2. In a medium bowl, mix together the coconut and sour cream until blended thoroughly.

3. Carefully fold in the drained oranges and pineapple chunks.

4. Serve immediately in individual dessert dishes or stemmed goblets. Garnish the top with the almonds or cherries. Keep any leftovers refrigerated.

5 TO 6 SERVINGS

BERRY-BANANA COMPOTE WITH TOASTED ALMONDS AND GRAPES

When you want a light, quick dessert, rely on in-season fresh fruits, varying them according to the calendar. Serve with cookies or biscotti.

⅓ cup slivered almonds
2 bananas
1 pint basket strawberries
1 cup green seedless grapes
3 tablespoons fresh orange juice or orange-flavored liqueur

1. Preheat the oven to 325 degrees F. Spread out the almonds in a small baking pan and bake 5 to 7 minutes, shaking the pan once or twice, until the nuts are lightly toasted. Immediately transfer to a plate to cool.

2. Meanwhile, peel and cut the bananas into slices. Rinse, hull and drain the strawberries. Slice the berries. Halve the grapes if you like.

3. In a medium bowl, combine the bananas, strawberries, grapes and orange juice. Toss to mix well. Divide the fruit mixture among 4 stemmed glasses or dessert dishes. Sprinkle the toasted almonds on top.

4 SERVINGS

MINTED CANTALOUPE

Dress up cantaloupe with a little mint flavoring. Be sure to use white crème de menthe rather than green for best appearance.

1 cantaloupe
3 tablespoons white crème de menthe
  Sweetened whipped cream (from a pressurized can)

1. Cut the cantaloupe crosswise in half. Scoop out and discard the seeds.

2. Using a melon baller, scoop out balls of cantaloupe and place in a medium bowl. Add the crème de menthe and toss well.

3. Place the cantaloupe balls and some of the liquid in stemmed goblets. Top with whipped cream and garnish with a mint leaf. Serve immediately.

2 TO 3 SERVINGS

MINTED STRAWBERRIES AND CANTALOUPE: Rinse, hull and halve 1 pint basket strawberries and add to melon balls in bowl. Proceed as directed above.

3 TO 4 SERVINGS

CITRUS CHERRY WINE COMPOTE

Dried cherries offer a tantalizing taste of this seasonal fruit even in the middle of winter. This compote is a simple finale to serve after a robust meal. In addition to flavor, the dried fruit adds an interesting, unexpected texture.

4 navel oranges, chilled
1 medium grapefruit, chilled
$1/2$ cup dried cherries
$1/2$ cup dry red wine (Burgundy is good)
$1/4$ cup sugar

1. Peel the oranges and divide into sections, removing any bitter white pith. Coarsely chop the oranges.

2. Peel the grapefruit and divide into sections, removing any bitter white pith. Coarsely chop the grapefruit.

3. In a medium bowl, combine the chopped oranges and grapefruit with the cherries, red wine and sugar. Stir to dissolve the sugar. Let stand 5 minutes.

4. Serve immediately or refrigerate until serving time.

4 TO 5 SERVINGS

FRESH FRUITS WITH ORANGE DIP

1 package (8 ounces) Neufchâtel (light) cream cheese,
   softened and cut up
⅓ cup orange juice
2 to 3 tablespoons powdered sugar
1 to 2 pint baskets fresh strawberries
2 cups melon chunks, pineapple chunks and/or fresh Bing
   cherries

1. In a food processor, blend the cream cheese until smooth. Add the orange juice and powdered sugar and process until smooth and thoroughly blended.

2. Rinse, hull and dry the strawberries.

3. Turn the cream cheese mixture into a serving dish. Place in the center of a serving platter. Surround with the strawberries and cut-up melon. Serve immediately. To eat, diners spoon some of the orange dip and fruits on to their dessert plates and dip the fruits into the sauce.

4 TO 6 SERVINGS

PINEAPPLE DIP: In step 1, instead of orange juice, add 1 can (8 ounces) crushed pineapple packed in juice. Add 2 to 3 tablespoons powdered sugar and ½ teaspoon ground ginger (optional) and process until smooth. Use 2 pints of strawberries and 3 cups of cut-up fruit. Proceed as directed above.

6 TO 8 SERVINGS

FRUIT TOPPED WITH LIME CREAM

For a refreshing change of pace, zip cut-up fresh fruits with a tangy lime-sour cream mixture. Vary the fruits according to the good buys at the produce stand or supermarket.

2 cups sliced fresh strawberries
2 cups peeled, cut-up fresh papaya or bananas or mango
3 tablespoons sugar
1 tablespoon plus 1 teaspoon fresh lime juice
$1/2$ cup sour cream

1. In a medium bowl, combine the strawberries, papaya, $1^{1/2}$ tablespoons of the sugar and 1 teaspoon of the lime juice, mixing well.

2. In a small bowl, mix together the remaining $1^{1/2}$ tablespoons sugar, the remaining 1 tablespoon lime juice and the sour cream.

3. Spoon the fruit mixture into 4 stemmed glasses or dessert dishes, dividing evenly. Top each with a dollop of the sour cream mixture. Serve immediately.

4 SERVINGS

LAYERED FRUIT SALAD WITH RASPBERRY TOPPING

The only thing that takes time here is cutting up the fruits, so save minutes by purchasing a melon already cut into chunks.

1 medium cantaloupe
2 pint baskets fresh strawberries
2 cups seedless green grapes
1 package (8 ounces) cream cheese, softened
1 container (8 ounces) raspberry yogurt

1. Cut the cantaloupe in half lengthwise. Scoop out and discard the seeds. Remove the cantaloupe from the rind and dice. Place the cut-up cantaloupe in the bottom of a 1½-quart glass bowl or clear glass serving dish or compote.

2. Rinse, drain and hull the strawberries. Cut them into slices. You should have about 4 cups. Reserve 1 cup. Layer the remaining strawberries on top of cantaloupe. Top with the green grapes.

3. Beat together the cream cheese and yogurt until smooth. Spread evenly over the top of the grapes. Arrange the remaining 1 cup strawberries attractively on top.

4 TO 5 SERVINGS

STRAWBERRY TOPPING: Instead of mixing cream cheese and raspberry yogurt for the topping, try the following. Mix 1 container (8 ounces) soft cream cheese with strawberries with 1 cup nonfat vanilla yogurt until smooth. Spoon evenly over the grapes and proceed as directed above.

TROPICAL FRUIT SALAD WITH TOASTED COCONUT

Busy cooks will welcome the convenience of toasting coconut quickly in the microwave oven.

1 ripe mango
2 large bananas
1 can (20 ounces) pineapple chunks packed in juice or
  2 cups fresh, diced pineapple chunks
2 tablespoons Grand Marnier or other orange-flavored
  liqueur
1/4 cup flaked coconut

1. Peel the mango. Slice the fruit from the pit and chop it into bite-size pieces. Place in a medium bowl. Slice the bananas and add to the bowl with the mango. Drain the pineapple chunks and add to the other fruit. Stir in the Grand Marnier.

2. Spread the coconut out on a double thickness of microwave-safe white paper towels in the microwave oven. Microwave on High for 1 minute; rearrange the coconut. Microwave on High for 1 minute longer, or until the coconut starts to turn golden brown.

3. Spoon the fruit into 4 stemmed glasses or dessert dishes. Sprinkle the toasted coconut on top.

4 SERVINGS

DRIED FRUIT COMPOTE

Served hot or warm, this is a comforting dessert for a cold night. A dollop of sour cream or vanilla yogurt can be added as topping. The dessert is delicious cold, too.

1 package (16 ounces) mixed dried fruit (prunes, peaches, apples, etc.)
3/4 cup fresh orange juice
1/4 cup packed brown sugar
2 cinnamon sticks
1/4 teaspoon grated nutmeg

1. In a 1½-quart glass bowl, combine the fruit, orange juice, brown sugar, cinnamon sticks and nutmeg. Cover with microwave-safe plastic wrap.

2. Microwave on High for 8 minutes, stirring twice and re-covering with the plastic wrap each time, until the fruit is soft. Remove the cinnamon sticks and discard.

3. Serve the fruit in dessert bowls with some of the cooking liquid.

4 SERVINGS

TROPICAL FRUIT SALSA

If you make the fruit salsa in advance of serving, be sure to keep it refrigerated. Substitute green grapes or chopped fresh nectarines for the bananas, if you prefer. Serve this over vanilla ice cream, frozen yogurt or pound cake.

1 pint basket strawberries
2 bananas
1 can (15¼ ounces) tropical fruit salad
½ cup chopped dates
3 to 4 tablespoons thawed frozen orange juice concentrate

1. Rinse, dry, hull and coarsely chop the strawberries. Place in a medium bowl. Peel and coarsely chop the bananas and add to the bowl.

2. Drain the fruit salad and add the drained fruit and chopped dates to the bowl. Stir in the orange juice concentrate.

3. Divide among 6 dessert dishes. Serve immediately.

6 SERVINGS

ORANGES WITH
COFFEE RICOTTA CREAM

Coffee and orange are terrific paired together, but if it doesn't appeal to you, I've added an all-orange option.

1 container (15 ounces) part-skim ricotta cheese
2/3 cup heavy cream
1/3 cup powdered sugar
1 teaspoon instant espresso coffee powder or 2 teaspoons grated orange zest
8 navel oranges

1. In a food processor, combine the ricotta cheese, cream, powdered sugar and espresso powder. Process until the mixture is creamy and as smooth as possible.

2. Peel the oranges and cut crosswise into ½-inch-thick slices. Arrange the slices, overlapping in a circle, on 8 dessert plates.

3. Spoon some of the ricotta mixture into the center of the oranges on each plate, dividing evenly, and serve.

8 SERVINGS

CHOCOLATE-SAUCED PEARS

1 cup white port wine
3 tablespoons sugar
4 ripe pears
1 cup semisweet chocolate chips (6 ounces)
1 teaspoon grated orange zest

1. In a 1½-quart glass casserole dish, combine the port and sugar. Stir to mix well.

2. Peel the pears and cut out the cores from the bottoms, but leave the stems intact. Place the pears in the port mixture (trim the bottoms if necessary, so they will stand up). Spoon some of the sweetened port over the pears to moisten them completely. Cover the dish tightly with microwave-safe plastic wrap. Microwave on High for 5 to 6 minutes, or until the pears are tender but not mushy when they are pierced with a fork.

3. In a 2-cup glass measure, combine ¼ cup of the pear cooking liquid with the chocolate chips. Microwave on High for 1 minute, or until the chocolate is melted and the sauce is smooth when whisked with a wire whisk. Stir in the orange zest.

4. To serve, place a generous 1½ tablespoons of the chocolate sauce in the center of each of 4 small dessert plates; tilt the plates so the sauce completely covers the bottom. Stand 1 well-drained pear upright in the center. Drizzle 1½ tablespoons of the chocolate sauce over each pear and serve.

4 SERVINGS

PEARS POACHED IN RED WINE

Be sure to use a good-quality Burgundy for best flavor. Some prefer serving the juices as is from the pan while others like to thicken them a little (mix 1 tablespoon cornstarch with 1 tablespoon cold water and stir into the wine liquid in the pan, cooking it until clear, bubbly and thickened), which yields a richer color sauce with a little more body.

    4 firm ripe pears
1¼ cups California red Burgundy wine
  ⅓ cup sugar
  ½ teaspoon ground cinnamon
    1 tablespoon lemon juice

1. Peel the pears, cut lengthwise in half and remove the cores. Cut each half lengthwise into 3 pieces.

2. In a large nonreactive frying pan, combine the wine, sugar and cinnamon. Heat to simmering over medium heat, stirring to dissolve the sugar. Add the pears to the hot spiced wine. Cover the pan and simmer 4 to 5 minutes, or until the pears are fork-tender but not mushy.

3. Stir in the lemon juice. Place the pear pieces in dessert dishes and spoon some of the hot wine liquid over them. Serve hot, at room temperature or chilled.

4 TO 5 SERVINGS

PEARS WITH DRIED CHERRIES AND GORGONZOLA

This is one of the most sophisticated ways to enjoy fruit and cheese for dessert. The combination of dried cherries, pears, red wine and Gorgonzola is a winner.

1/2 cup ruby port or Burgundy wine
1/2 cup dried cherries
 2 Bosc pears or Granny Smith apples
3/4 cup crumbled good-quality Gorgonzola cheese

1. In a small glass bowl or 1-cup measure, combine the port and cherries. Microwave on High for 1 to 1½ minutes, or until the liquid is hot and bubbly and the cherries are soft.

2. Cut the pears lengthwise in half. Scoop out the cores and cut each half lengthwise into slices. Fan out the slices on 4 dessert plates, dividing evenly.

3. Spoon the cherries and port over the pear slices. Sprinkle 3 tablespoons of the crumbled cheese over each serving.

4 SERVINGS

Pear Slices with Blue Cheese Spread

When you want to serve fruit and cheese for dessert or in a buffet, whip up this festive spread on a moment's notice with cream cheese, blue cheese and chopped pecans. If you prepare it ahead, brush the pear slices with lemon juice so they don't turn brown.

1/3 cup chopped pecans
2 packages (8 ounces each) cream cheese, softened
1/2 cup heavy cream
3/4 cup crumbled Danish blue cheese
8 to 10 ripe, firm Bosc or Bartlett pears

1. Place the pecans in a small glass bowl or dish. Microwave on High for 1 to 1 1/2 minutes, or until they are toasted; set aside.

2. In a medium bowl with an electric mixer on medium speed, beat the cream cheese until smooth. With the mixer on low speed, beat in the cream. With the mixer on medium speed, beat 2 to 3 minutes, until light and fluffy. Beat in the blue cheese until smooth.

3. Turn the spread into an attractive serving dish, such as a 6 1/2-by-2 1/2-inch soufflé dish; smooth the top. Sprinkle the toasted pecans over the cheese spread.

4. Cut the fruit into 1/4- to 1/2-inch slices. Place the serving dish with the blue cheese spread in the center of a large platter and arrange the pear slices around it.

8 OR MORE SERVINGS

PINEAPPLE MELBA DESSERT

This is the utmost in simplicity but it tastes wonderful. Cutting and presenting the pineapple attractively goes a long way to making this dessert eye appealing. The combination of pineapple and raspberries is hard to beat.

1 fresh pineapple
2 to 3 cups fresh or thawed frozen raspberries
2 to 3 tablespoons powdered sugar
$1/3$ cup orange juice
6 tablespoons vanilla yogurt or frozen yogurt

1. Remove the pineapple crown, if desired. Cut the pineapple in half lengthwise, then cut each half into 3 lengthwise wedges. Cut the pineapple from the shell lengthwise in one piece; leave the fruit sitting on the pineapple shell. Then cut each long wedge of pineapple crosswise into $1/2$-inch pieces. Push one pineapple piece from the shell to the right (out about $1/2$ to 1-inch) and the next piece to the left, alternating until all pieces are pushed out a little for an attractive decorative presentation.

2. In a medium bowl, combine the raspberries, powdered sugar and orange juice. Stir to mix well.

3. To serve, place a pineapple wedge (on the shell) on a dessert plate. Spoon the raspberry mixture over the pineapple wedges. Top with a dollop of yogurt and serve.

6 SERVINGS

Raspberries with Quick Creme Fraiche

When you want an elegant dessert pronto, try this. You can top almost any fresh fruit with the cream.

1/2 cup heavy cream
1/2 cup sour cream
1 tablespoon sugar
1 teaspoon grated orange zest (optional)
3 cups fresh raspberries, rinsed and drained, or fresh strawberries, rinsed, drained and hulled

1. In a small bowl, whisk together the cream and sour cream until smooth.

2. Whisk in the sugar and orange zest, if desired, until the sugar dissolves.

3. Divide the raspberries evenly among 4 or 6 stemmed goblets or dessert dishes.

4. Top with some of the cream mixture, dividing evenly. Garnish each serving with a mint leaf, if desired. Serve immediately.

4 to 6 servings

NOTE: The cream mixture can also be used to top other fresh fruits such as oranges, pineapple, papaya, etc.

STRAWBERRIES IN BALSAMIC VINEGAR

Don't turn up your nose until you taste this interesting Italian-inspired combination. It's wonderful. The mild tartness of the vinegar highlights the flavor of the strawberries. Serve with amaretti or biscotti on the side.

    1 pint basket fresh strawberries
1½ to 2 tablespoons sugar (depending on the sweetness of the berries)
    2 teaspoons balsamic vinegar (available at supermarkets or Italian markets)

1. Rinse, drain, hull and slice the strawberries. Place in a small bowl.

2. Stir in the sugar and let stand 5 minutes.

3. Stir in the balsamic vinegar. Serve immediately.

2 SERVINGS

STRAWBERRIES WITH MASCARPONE CREAM

Mascarpone cheese adds a special touch to the strawberries and cream in this dessert.

2 pint baskets fresh strawberries
$1/2$ cup heavy cream
3 tablespoons powdered sugar
1 teaspoon vanilla extract
$1/2$ cup mascarpone cheese

1. Rinse, dry and hull strawberries. Reserve 4 whole berries for garnish. Cut the remaining berries into bite-size pieces. Divide evenly among 4 stemmed dessert glasses or dishes.

2. In a medium bowl with an electric mixer on high speed, beat the cream with the sugar and vanilla to almost stiff peaks. With the mixer on low speed, beat in the mascarpone cheese until blended.

3. Spoon one-fourth of the cheese mixture on top of the berries in each dish. Garnish each with a whole reserved strawberry.

4 SERVINGS

STRAWBERRIES ROMANOFF

When fresh strawberries are at their best, a simple dessert, such as this classic, is often the best choice. Serve with store-bought butter cookies or shortbread.

2 pint baskets fresh strawberries
1/4 cup plus 2 tablespoons sugar
1/3 cup orange juice
3 tablespoons Grand Marnier or Curacao
1 cup heavy cream

1. Rinse, drain and hull the strawberries. Quarter the berries or cut them into slices and place them in a medium bowl.

2. Sprinkle 1/4 cup of the sugar over the berries and toss gently. Pour on the orange juice and 2 tablespoons of the Grand Marnier. Let stand, tossing several times, until serving time.

3. Shortly before serving, in a medium bowl with an electric mixer on high speed, beat the cream to soft peaks. Add the remaining 2 tablespoons sugar and 1 tablespoon Grand Marnier and beat to stiff peaks.

4. Spoon the strawberry mixture into 6 stemmed glasses, dividing evenly. Top with the whipped cream.

6 SERVINGS

Pineapple with Kirsch

The ultimate in simplicity, but sophisticated and delicious.

1 medium to large fresh pineapple
²/₃ cup kirsch
Sugar (optional)

1. Slice the top and bottom off the pineapple. Stand up and cut off the outer shell and all eyes.

2. Cut the pineapple into ½-inch slices and place in a wide, shallow bowl or container. Pour the kirsch over the pineapple. If the pineapple is not completely ripe, sweeten with sugar to taste. Let stand at room temperature 1 to 2 hours. Cover and refrigerate if you prefer the pineapple chilled.

3. Place 1 or 2 slices on each of 6 serving plates. Spoon the kirsch over the pineapple and serve with a knife and fork.

6 SERVINGS

7 Ice Cream and Other Frozen Desserts

This is the chapter to turn to when you're in the mood for cool, frosty desserts. They're an ideal way to beat the heat during the summer months. Here's the scoop. Some of the recipes call for advance preparation of ten minutes or less but require time in the freezer, while others are prepared and served immediately. If you don't want to be bustling around the kitchen making dessert just prior to serving time, choose a dessert that needs freezing.

Many of these desserts mix and match store-bought ice cream with purchased ingredients, such as crumb crusts, cakes, brownies, cookies, waffles and the like. Using some prepared products is a must if you want to save the most time, but keep up your standards of quality by choosing only the best.

Keep in mind that ice cream will lose some of its volume with repeated handling. Therefore, work quickly and allow the ice cream to soften only slightly (in the refrigerator). The quickest and easiest way to layer ice cream in a crust or pan is to buy it in a paper container; with a sharp knife, cut away the carton and cut the ice cream into large hunks, slices or pieces to fit.

Also remember that for ease in cutting and optimum flavor, the finished frozen desserts often require ten to fifteen minutes thawing time in the refrigerator or at room temperature prior to serving.

APRICOT-COCONUT SUNDAES

Whip this up on a moment's notice for apricot lovers. The sauce relies on apricot preserves and a little cream.

$1/2$ cup apricot preserves
$1/2$ cup heavy cream
1 teaspoon butter
$1^1/2$ pints rich vanilla ice cream
6 tablespoons shredded coconut

1. In a small saucepan, mix together the apricot preserves, cream and butter. Heat to boiling over medium-high heat, stirring often. Reduce the heat to medium and cook, stirring occasionally, until the mixture thickens slightly, 4 to 5 minutes.

2. Place a scoop of the ice cream in each of 6 dessert dishes. Spoon the warm apricot sauce over the ice cream, dividing evenly.

3. Sprinkle 1 tablespoon of the coconut over each sundae.

6 SERVINGS

SUNNY APRICOT SUNDAES

This apricot sauce made with dried apricots and apricot nectar is dynamite. For a pretty presentation, layer the ice cream and sauce in parfait glasses. And if butter pecan is not your favorite flavor ice cream, feel free to substitute one that is.

1½ cups dried apricots
1 can (12 ounces) apricot nectar
¼ cup sugar
3 tablespoons Cognac or brandy
1 to 1½ quarts butter pecan ice cream

1. In a 1-quart glass measure or bowl, combine the apricots, apricot nectar and sugar. Cover with microwave-safe plastic wrap. Microwave on High for 5 to 6 minutes, or until the apricots are tender.

2. Transfer to a food processor and puree until the sauce is as smooth as possible. Add the Cognac and process until mixed.

3. To serve, scoop the ice cream into 6 to 8 stemmed glasses or dessert dishes. Top with the warm apricot sauce and serve.

6 TO 8 SERVINGS

BANANA WAFFLE SUNDAES

Here's a delicious flavor combination that's guaranteed to be a big hit with the kids.

¼ cup chunky peanut butter
½ cup bottled caramel flavor ice cream topping or chocolate
   fudge ice cream topping
 4 store-bought waffles
 2 bananas
 1 pint vanilla ice cream

1. In a 2-cup glass measure, combine the peanut butter and caramel topping. Microwave on High for 1 to 1½ minutes, or until warm and the mixture is well blended when stirred.

2. Warm and crisp the waffles in a toaster or toaster oven. Peel and slice the bananas.

3. For each serving, place a warm waffle on a dessert plate. Top with a scoop of the ice cream and slices from half a banana. Spoon one-fourth of the caramel-peanut butter sauce on top of each and serve at once.

4 SERVINGS

BUTTERSCOTCH SUNDAES

This sauce is also yummy over sliced bananas, sliced fresh peaches or other fruits instead of ice cream. If you can afford a sixth ingredient, garnish these sundaes with chopped pecans.

```
 3 tablespoons butter
3/4 cup heavy cream
 1 cup packed brown sugar
 1 teaspoon vanilla extract
11/2 pints ice cream
```

1. In a medium saucepan, melt the butter over medium heat. Stir in the cream and brown sugar. Heat to boiling over high heat; reduce the heat to medium-high and cook, stirring occasionally, until thickened, 3 to 4 minutes. Stir in the vanilla. Cool a few minutes.

2. Place a scoop of the ice cream in each of 6 dessert dishes or bowls. Spoon the sauce over the ice cream and serve.

6 SERVINGS

CHOCOLATE PEANUT BUTTER ICE CREAM PIE

This tastes like a giant peanut butter cup.

1½ quarts French vanilla ice cream
2 cups chopped milk chocolate pieces
¾ cup chunky peanut butter, at room temperature
¾ cup heavy cream

1. Scoop the ice cream into a medium bowl and set out to soften at room temperature for 5 minutes.

2. Meanwhile, sprinkle 1 cup of the chocolate pieces evenly over the bottom of a 9-inch pie pan.

3. Add the peanut butter to the softened vanilla ice cream and quickly mix with a spoon until blended. Whisk in the unwhipped cream until thoroughly mixed.

4. Turn the ice cream mixture into the pie pan. Sprinkle the remaining 1 cup chocolate pieces over the top. Cover with plastic wrap and freeze until firm, 3 to 4 hours.

8 TO 10 SERVINGS

CRANBERRY RASPBERRY PARFAITS

If you have cranberries stashed in the freezer, you can make this colorful dessert year-round. Otherwise you'll have to wait for the holidays when cranberries are in season.

> 1 package (12 ounces) fresh or frozen cranberries (3 cups)
> 1½ cups packed light brown sugar
> ½ cup orange juice
> 2 to 3 tablespoons Grand Marnier
> 2 pints raspberry sorbet

1. Rinse the cranberries well. Pick them over for foreign pieces, discard any bad berries and drain well.

2. In a 3-quart nonreactive saucepan, combine the cranberries, brown sugar and orange juice. Heat to boiling over medium-high heat. Cook until the cranberry skins pop, 4 to 6 minutes. Remove from the heat and stir in the Grand Marnier.

3. Layer the sorbet and cranberry sauce in 8 parfait dishes or stemmed glasses. Serve at once.

8 SERVINGS

ESPRESSO TORTONI

An adaptation of an Italian-American idea. Prepare before you sit down to dinner and stash in the freezer. For ease in eating, this dessert is best served partially frozen rather than rock hard.

1½ cups heavy cream
  3 tablespoons powdered sugar
  4 teaspoons instant espresso powder
  2 tablespoons coffee-flavored liqueur, such as Kahlúa
  ½ cup plus 2 tablespoons crushed amaretti, Italian
    macaroons

1. In a medium bowl with an electric mixer on low speed, beat the cream, powdered sugar and espresso powder until well blended. Increase the mixer speed to high and beat until the cream mixture forms stiff but soft peaks.

2. Stir in the coffee liqueur and ½ cup of the macaroon crumbs, mixing until evenly blended. Turn the mixture into 6 individual, double-paper muffin cups or 6 freezerproof dessert dishes. Sprinkle the remaining 2 tablespoons macaroon crumbs over the tops.

3. Freeze 1 to 1½ hours, or until partially set but not frozen firm.

6 SERVINGS

LEMON ICE RING WITH FRESH BERRIES AND VODKA

Unmold and serve this attractive lemon sorbet ring filled with fresh blueberries and strawberries. Drizzle with vodka at the table to impress the most discriminating guests.

2 pints lemon sorbet
2 cups fresh blueberries or blackberries
2 cups fresh strawberries
2 to 3 tablespoons sugar
1/3 cup vodka or Triple Sec

1. Soften the sorbet a few minutes at room temperature or microwave on High for 15 to 20 seconds. Press the softened sorbet firmly and evenly into a 5- to 6-cup ring mold. Freeze the ring mold for 2 to 3 hours, or until firm.

2. Rinse and drain the blueberries. Rinse the strawberries; dry, hull and quarter them. In a medium bowl, mix together the blueberries, strawberries and sugar. Cover and refrigerate until serving time.

3. To serve, unmold the lemon sorbet ring onto a round platter by dipping the mold quickly in very hot water, running a knife around the inside edge and inverting it onto the platter. Pile the berries inside the ring. Drizzle the vodka over the sorbet. Slice the sorbet ring into pieces and serve immediately topped with the fresh fruits and some of the juices.

8 SERVINGS

PAPAYA ORANGE FRAPPE SUNDAES WITH BERRY SAUCE

Papayas have a bright orange color that is particularly attractive with bright berries. Be sure your papayas are ripe, or the dessert will not be sweet enough.

2 ripe fresh papayas
1 package (16 ounces) frozen mixed berries, partially thawed
1/3 cup powdered sugar
2 tablespoons fresh lime juice
1 quart orange sherbet

1. Cut the papayas in half lengthwise, peel the fruit and discard the seeds. Then cut into small crosswise slices or chop into 1-inch chunks.

2. In a food processor fitted with a metal blade, process the berries, powdered sugar and lime juice until all of the berries are pureed. Strain through a fine sieve to remove the seeds, if you like.

3. Divide the papayas among 8 stemmed goblets. Top with 1 large or 2 small scoops of the sherbet in each. Spoon on the berry sauce, dividing evenly, and serve.

8 SERVINGS

PEACH-BERRY MELBA

Peaches and berries team in this refreshing finish.

8 soft macaroon cookies
1½ cups fresh raspberries or blueberries
2 large fresh peaches
2 tablespoons orange juice
1 pint vanilla ice cream

1. Crumble the cookies into crumbs. Rinse and drain the berries. Set on paper towels to dry.

2. Peel the peaches by submerging them in boiling water for 30 seconds. Rinse under cold water and slide off the skins. Slice the peaches.

3. In a food processor, combine the berries and orange juice. Process until the mixture is pureed and smooth.

4. Spoon 2 tablespoons of the macaroon crumbs into the bottom of each of 4 dessert dishes. Divide the peach slices evenly among the dessert dishes.

5. Place a scoop of ice cream over the peaches in each dish. Spoon the berry puree over the ice cream. Serve immediately.

4 SERVINGS

QUICK PEACH FROZEN YOGURT

When you want something sweet but can't afford a lot of calories, try this dessert reminiscent of frozen yogurt. You won't believe you can make something so tasty with frozen peaches and yogurt. To keep the calories in check, sweeten with a little sugar substitute instead of sugar.

1 bag (16 ounces) frozen unsweetened sliced peaches (do not thaw)
1 cup peach or vanilla yogurt
2 to 3 tablespoons powdered sugar, to taste
½ teaspoon vanilla extract

1. Set aside a few peach slices for garnish. In a food processor, chop the remaining frozen peaches.

2. Add the yogurt and process until as smooth as possible, scraping down the sides of the bowl once or twice. Add the sugar and vanilla and mix until blended.

3. Serve immediately in stemmed glasses, garnished with the reserved peach slices.

3 TO 4 SERVINGS

PEACH AND RASPBERRY FROZEN DELIGHT

1 bag (16 ounces) frozen unsweetened sliced peaches (do not thaw)
2 cups heavy cream
1/4 cup powdered sugar
1 bag (12 ounces) frozen unsweetened raspberries (do not thaw)

1. In a food processor, process the frozen peaches until finely chopped. Add 1 cup of the cream and 2 tablespoons powdered sugar and process until the mixture is pureed and smooth, scraping down the sides of the bowl a couple of times with a rubber spatula. Remove the mixture to a bowl and set aside while making the raspberry mixture.

2. In the same food processor bowl (it is not necessary to rinse it out), process the frozen raspberries until finely chopped. Add the remaining 1 cup cream and the remaining 2 tablespoons powdered sugar and process until the mixture is pureed and as smooth as possible, scraping down the sides of the bowl a couple of times with a rubber spatula.

3. Quickly place a scoop or large spoonful of each of the peach and raspberry frozen mixtures into each of 8 stemmed dessert glasses. Serve immediately. Freeze any leftovers.

8 SERVINGS

PEARS BELLE HELENE

Keep canned pears, ice cream and fudge topping on hand, and you have the makings for this easy adaptation of the French dessert classic.

2 cans (16 ounces each) or 1 can (29 ounces) Bartlett pear
　　halves (if using this size can you'll have only
　　7 pear halves rather than 8 total from the two cans) packed
　　in syrup
1 pint vanilla ice cream
$\frac{1}{2}$ to $\frac{3}{4}$ cup chocolate fudge topping
4 candied violets or sprigs of fresh mint, for garnish

1. Drain the pears well.

2. Scoop the ice cream into 4 dessert dishes and press 2 pear halves, rounded sides out, into each ice cream scoop on opposite sides so that the pears stand up.

3. Place the fudge topping in a glass dish. Microwave on High for 35 to 45 seconds, or until warm and smooth when stirred. Spoon the sauce over the pears and ice cream, dividing evenly. Garnish with candied violets or mint, if you like. Serve immediately.

4 SERVINGS

QUICK RASPBERRY SORBET

You won't believe how easily this creamy frozen sorbet-style dessert goes together. Even better it's a terrific choice for those watching their weight—and they'll probably never guess it contains yogurt. It's best served immediately after making.

2 seedless oranges
1 bag (12 ounces) frozen unsweetened raspberries
   (do not thaw)
3/4 cup nonfat vanilla yogurt

1. Peel one of the oranges; coarsely chop. Cut the other orange in half and squeeze enough juice to yield 1/4 cup.

2. In a food processor, combine the chopped orange, orange juice, frozen raspberries and yogurt. Process until well blended and as smooth as possible.

3. Serve immediately in dessert dishes or stemmed glasses. Or freeze for a short time and serve later. If frozen solid, microwave on Defrost or Low for 1 to 2 minutes, or until just soft enough to serve.

4 SERVINGS

RASPBERRY SORBET WITH PEACHES AND CHOCOLATE

For an impressive, elegant-looking dessert, present this combination. Arrange the sorbet in the center of the plate and surround with peach slices radiating out in a circular pattern from the center. Drizzle the works with chocolate sauce. The flavor is outstanding

2 fresh peaches
3/4 cup semisweet chocolate chips
3 tablespoons milk
1 pint raspberry sorbet

1. Peel, halve and pit the peaches. Cut the fruit into 1/4-inch-thick slices. Place one-fourth of the peach slices on each of 4 dessert plates in a spoke pattern radiating from the center.

2. In a 1-cup glass measure, combine the chocolate chips and the milk. Microwave on High for 1 to 1 1/4 minutes, or until the chocolate is melted and smooth when stirred.

3. Place a scoop of the sorbet in the center of each plate on top of the peach slices. With a back and forth motion, drizzle the chocolate sauce on top of the peaches and sorbet, making an attractive-looking pattern. Serve immediately.

4 SERVINGS

TOFU RASPBERRY FREEZE

You won't believe this frosty treat is made with tofu. It's a dieter's delight and delicious! This is best served as soon as it is made.

1 bag (12 ounces) frozen unsweetened red raspberries
   (do not thaw)
1 cup drained soft tofu
1 teaspoon vanilla extract
3 tablespoons sugar

1. In a food processor, combine the frozen raspberries (straight from the freezer), tofu, vanilla and 1 tablespoon sugar. Process until pureed and well blended, scraping down the sides of the bowl, if necessary.

2. Taste and add the additional sugar if you think it is needed.

3. Serve immediately in individual stemmed glasses or dessert dishes.

3 TO 4 SERVINGS

ICED STRAWBERRY CREAM

This frozen dessert is divine, with a taste that's a cross between ice cream and yogurt, only better.

1 bag (16 ounces) frozen unsweetened whole strawberries (do not thaw)
$\frac{1}{2}$ cup nonfat vanilla or strawberry yogurt
$\frac{1}{2}$ cup heavy cream
1 to 2 tablespoons powdered sugar
$\frac{1}{2}$ teaspoon vanilla extract

1. In a food processor, process the frozen strawberries until chopped up.

2. Add the yogurt and cream and process until smooth and thoroughly blended.

3. Add 1 tablespoon of the powdered sugar and the vanilla. Process until blended. Taste and add the additional tablespoon sugar if you think it is needed.

4. Spoon the strawberry cream into stemmed goblets and serve at once.

4 SERVINGS

TROPICAL MANGO YOGURT COUPES

When mangoes are in season, try this refreshing sauce made with lime juice. Try serving the sauce on various fruit-flavored yogurts and sorbets.

1 mango
2 tablespoons powdered sugar
1 tablespoon fresh lime juice
1 pint raspberry or vanilla frozen yogurt
3 tablespoons shredded coconut

1. Peel the mango. Cut the fruit from the seed, discard the seed and place the mango in a food processor.

2. Add the powdered sugar and lime juice. Process until the mango is pureed and the sauce is as smooth as possible.

3. Place a scoop of the frozen yogurt in each of 4 dessert dishes. Spoon one-fourth of the mango sauce over each serving of yogurt. Sprinkle the coconut on top.

4 SERVINGS

Tropical Fruit on Ice

This light and refreshing combination is welcome after a heavy meal or on a hot day. A pint basket of strawberries can be substituted for the papaya.

1 mango
3 kiwifruit
1 papaya
Juice of 1 small lime
1½ pints lime sorbet

1. Peel the mango and cut it into ¼- to ½-inch dice. Discard the pit. Place in a medium bowl. Peel and dice the kiwifruit. Add to the bowl with the mango.

2. Peel the papaya, cut it in half and scoop out and discard the seeds. Dice the papaya. Add to the bowl with the other fruit.

3. Sprinkle the lime juice over the fruit and toss to mix.

4. Place 1 scoop of the sorbet in each of 6 dessert dishes; spoon some of the fruit mixture over the top, dividing evenly. Serve immediately.

6 SERVINGS

FROZEN YOGURT FRUIT POPS

These are favorite treats with the young set.

2 cups frozen unsweetened whole strawberries or raspberries
1 carton (8 ounces) vanilla lowfat or nonfat yogurt
1 to 2 tablespoons powdered sugar

1. In a food processor fitted with a metal blade, process the berries until finely chopped.

2. Add the yogurt and powdered sugar and process until smooth.

3. Divide the mixture evenly among 5 (5-ounce) paper cups. Cover the foil, make a slit in the center of the foil with a knife tip and insert a wooden stick or a sturdy plastic spoon through the foil into each cup.

4. Freeze until firm, at least 2 to 3 hours. At serving time, tear away the paper and eat.

MAKES 5 FROZEN POPS

FRESH FRUIT YOGURT POPS: Instead of 2 cups frozen berries, combine 1 cup pureed fresh fruit (use any combination of strawberries, peeled peaches, nectarines, apricots and bananas) with 1 carton (8 ounces) vanilla or a fruit-flavored yogurt and sugar as directed above. Proceed as directed; freeze.

8 COOKIES, CANDIES, DRINKS AND SAUCES

If you're looking for a smaller sweet option, peruse the fuss-free sampler that follows. Recipes run the gamut from fudge, rocky road and other confections to warm and cold dessert beverages. An array of tempting sauces to serve over cakes, waffles, ice cream and fruit includes Chocolate Peanut Butter Sauce, Boysenberry White Chocolate Topping, Jiffy Pineapple-Orange Sauce, Peachy Keen Sauce and more.

You'll welcome yummy little nibbles like Apricot Coconut Balls, prepared simply by mixing together dried apricots, coconut, sweetened condensed milk and finely chopped chocolate and shaping the mélange into small rounds. Or Peanut Butter Balls, turned out with peanut butter, sugar and cream.

Kids will adore the Quick Peanut Butter Cookie Sandwiches, Pretzel Peanut Chocolate Candies and Banana Yogurt Shake. They may even want to lend a helping hand to make them for their own snacks.

For a lift any time, try the Iced Mocha or the Chococoffee Pick-Me-Up. They're a cinch to zap out with a little assistance from the food processor or microwave oven.

JIFFY PEANUT BUTTER AND DATE COOKIES

These flourless confections are a cross between cookies and candy. Kids love them.

1 cup chunky peanut butter
3/4 cup sugar
1 egg
1 teaspoon vanilla extract
1/4 cup finely chopped dates

1. Preheat the oven to 350 degrees F. In a medium bowl, combine the peanut butter, sugar, egg and vanilla. Mix until well blended. Stir in the dates.

2. Drop by teaspoonfuls 2 inches apart on ungreased cookie sheets. Flatten the dough in a crisscross pattern with the tines of a fork.

3. Bake for 8 to 10 minutes, or until golden. Remove to racks to cool.

MAKES ABOUT 4 DOZEN COOKIES

CHOCOLATE CHUNK COOKIES

A good bet, these go together effortlessly. Use white chocolate chunks or bittersweet or semisweet chocolate.

    6 tablespoons butter, softened
    3/4 cup packed brown sugar
    1 egg
    1 1/2 cups flour
    6 ounces imported white chocolate or bittersweet or
        semisweet chocolate, cut into 1/2-inch pieces

1. Preheat the oven to 350 degrees F. Meanwhile, in a medium bowl with an electric mixer on medium speed, beat together the butter, brown sugar and egg until light and fluffy.

2. Beat in the flour until thoroughly blended. By hand, stir in the chocolate pieces.

3. Using a small scoop or generous rounded tablespoonfuls, drop mounds of the dough 2 inches apart on ungreased cookie sheets. Flatten the dough with your fingertips into 2 1/2-inch rounds.

4. Bake the cookies for 9 to 10 minutes, or until light golden around the edges. Do not overbake. Let the cookies cool a few minutes on the pan before removing to a rack to cool completely.

MAKES ABOUT 16 COOKIES

QUICK PEANUT BUTTER COOKIE SANDWICHES

These are perfect for kids' parties or snacks. Oatmeal or chocolate chip cookies can be used in place of the chocolate wafers.

16 chocolate wafer cookies
1/3 cup chunky peanut butter
1/2 cup semisweet chocolate chips
1 1/2 teaspoons vegetable oil

1. Sandwich 2 of the cookies together with some of the peanut butter in between. Smooth the edges with a knife, if necessary. Repeat with the remaining cookies and peanut butter.

2. Meanwhile, in a small glass bowl, combine the chocolate chips and oil. Microwave on High for 1 to 1 1/2 minutes, stirring twice, until the chocolate is melted and smooth when stirred.

3. Dip each of the filled cookies halfway into the chocolate mixture or spread the chocolate over half of each cookie, front and back, with a knife. Place on a wax paper-lined jelly-roll pan.

4. Refrigerate until the chocolate is set, about 8 to 10 minutes.

MAKES 8 FILLED COOKIES

BUTTERY ORANGE CHOCOLATE CHIP COOKIES

Since these contain no eggs, they bake in minutes. Dust the tops with additional powdered sugar while warm, if desired.

    1 orange
    12 tablespoons (1 1/2 sticks) butter
    3/4 cup powdered sugar
    1 1/2 cups flour
    1 cup semisweet chocolate chips (6 ounces)

1. Preheat the oven to 375 degrees F. Grate the colored zest and squeeze 2 teaspoons juice from the orange.

2. In a medium bowl with an electric mixer on medium speed, beat together the butter, powdered sugar, 2 teaspoons of the orange zest and 2 teaspoons orange juice until light and fluffy. Add the flour and beat until well blended. The dough will be stiff (if it is too crumbly, press it together with your fingers). Stir in the chocolate chips.

3. Drop the dough by teaspoonfuls 2 inches apart onto 2 ungreased baking sheets; press the tops of the cookies slightly with your fingertips to flatten.

4. Bake 8 to 10 minutes, or until the edges begin to brown lightly. Remove to racks to cool. While warm, sift additional powdered sugar over the tops, if you like.

MAKES ABOUT 30 COOKIES

CHOCOLATE CHIP
COCONUT MACAROONS

If coconut macaroons are your passion, these chewy cookies should be a favorite. Upon occasion, try substituting 1½ cups chopped pecans for the chocolate chips.

    1 can (14 ounces) sweetened condensed milk
    4 cups shredded coconut
    2 teaspoons vanilla extract
    ½ cup flour
1½ cups semisweet chocolate chips (9 ounces)

1. Preheat the oven to 350 degrees F. In a medium bowl, mix together the sweetened condensed milk, coconut and vanilla until well blended. Add the flour and blend well. Stir in the chocolate chips.

2. Drop the mixture by teaspoonfuls 2 inches apart onto greased, foil-lined cookie sheets.

3. Bake 8 to 9 minutes, or until golden brown on the edges. Let the cookies cool on the sheets. Carefully remove from the foil.

MAKES 4 DOZEN COOKIES

PECAN CHOCOLATE PASTRY ROLLUPS

1 package (17¼ ounces) frozen puff pastry (2 sheets)
1 cup chopped pecans
⅔ cup miniature semisweet chocolate chips
   Powdered sugar

1. Preheat the oven to 425 degrees F. Thaw the pastry as directed on the package, but be sure it is still cold.

2. With a rolling pin, on a floured pastry cloth or work surface, one at a time roll out each pastry sheet to a 10-by-14-inch rectangle. Sprinkle ½ cup of the pecans and ⅓ cup of the chocolate chips over each pastry sheet to within ¾ inch of the edges. With your fingertips, press the pecans and chips lightly into the pastry.

3. Moisten the edge of the long side of the pastry farthest away from you with a little water. Roll up the pastry from the long side closest to you, jelly-roll fashion, pressing in the moistened edge of the dough to seal.

4. Place each roll, 3 inches apart, seam-side down, on an ungreased baking sheet. Using a sharp knife, carefully cut each roll crosswise into 1-inch slices, separating the slices slightly but leaving them standing upright next to each other.

5. Bake for 9 to 10 minutes, or until light golden. Sift powdered sugar lightly over the tops. Serve while warm.

MAKES 26 TO 28 SMALL PASTRIES

CHOCOLATE COCONUT CHEWS

There's hardly a cookie you can make and bake within 10 minutes; this is as close as it comes. They were a big hit with my children.

1 package (12 ounces) semisweet chocolate chips
1 can (14 ounces) sweetened condensed milk
2 teaspoons vanilla extract
⅔ cup flour
1 to 1½ cups shredded coconut or chopped pecans

1. Preheat the oven to 350 degrees F.

2. In a medium glass bowl, combine the chocolate chips and sweetened condensed milk. Microwave on High for 1½ to 1¾ minutes, or until the chocolate is melted and smooth when stirred. Stir in the vanilla until thoroughly blended. Stir in the flour, mixing well, and then the coconut.

3. Drop the dough by heaping teaspoonfuls 2 inches apart onto greased, foil-lined cookie sheets. Bake 8 to 9 minutes; the cookies will be dull on top and soft. Let cool on the cookie sheets; then carefully remove from the foil.

MAKES 46 COOKIES

CHOCOLATE RASPBERRY BISCUITS

When you want a little something tempting to munch on with hot coffee, try these instant sweet rolls.

 1 package (7.5 ounces) refrigerator biscuits
 5 teaspoons seedless red raspberry jam
10 teaspoons miniature semisweet chocolate chips
 1 tablespoon sugar

1. Preheat the oven to 425 degrees F. Line a large baking sheet with a piece of foil.

2. Remove the biscuits from the package and separate them. On the foil-lined baking pan, pat out each biscuit into a 4-inch circle by pressing with your fingertips.

3. Spread ½ teaspoon jam on half of each biscuit round. Top the jam with 1 teaspoon chocolate chips. Fold the biscuit in half to enclose the filling and form a half circle. Using a fork, press the edges together to seal. Repeat with the other biscuits.

4. Sprinkle the granulated sugar over the tops of the biscuits. Bake on the middle rack of the oven for 8 to 9 minutes, or until golden brown, watching carefully to be sure they don't burn. Serve warm.

MAKES 10 SWEET BISCUITS

CINNAMON S'MORES

A favorite with the young set. Let them try their hand at assembling this dessert treat.

 8 large marshmallows
16 cinnamon graham cracker squares
 2 (1.55-ounce) milk chocolate candy bars

1. Preheat the oven broiler. Cut the marshmallows horizontally in half.

2. Place 8 of the graham cracker squares, cinnamon side-up, on a foil-lined jelly-roll pan. Top each with one-fourth of a candy bar and then with 2 of the marshmallow halves, cut-sides down.

3. Broil 6 to 7 inches from the heat for 1 to 1¼ minutes, until the tops of the marshmallows are golden brown. Watch carefully to avoid burning.

4. Remove from the oven and top each S'more with another graham cracker square, pressing down lightly on the marshmallows. Serve immediately, allowing 2 per person.

4 SERVINGS

PEANUT BUTTER AND WHITE CHOCOLATE PRETZELS

Kids give these top marks for a dessert treat. For fun, sprinkle the tops of the pretzels immediately after coating with miniature chocolate chips or colored sprinkles so they'll adhere as the coating sets.

1/4 cup smooth peanut butter
3/4 cup chopped imported white chocolate (about 3 1/2 ounces)
35 to 40 mini pretzels (about 1 1/2 by 1 1/2 inches)

1. In a medium glass bowl, combine the peanut butter and white chocolate. Microwave on Medium for 2 minutes; stir well. Microwave on High for 1 to 1 1/2 minutes, or until the mixture is melted and smooth when stirred.

2. Place 5 to 6 pretzels at a time in the melted white chocolate and turn carefully with a fork to coat. Remove one at a time with a fork, tapping on the edge of the bowl to remove the excess chocolate mixture.

3. Place the coated pretzels on a wax paper-lined jelly-roll pan. Refrigerate at least 20 to 30 minutes, until firm. Store, covered, in the refrigerator.

MAKES 35 TO 40 PRETZELS

APRICOT COCONUT BALLS

These are a breeze to throw together. Rolled in powdered sugar or ground chocolate, they provide instant gratification.

1 package (7 ounces) dried apricots
2 cups shredded coconut
$1/2$ cup sweetened condensed milk
$1/2$ cup finely chopped semisweet or milk chocolate or miniature semisweet chocolate chips (optional)
   Sifted powdered sugar or sweetened cocoa powder

1. Finely chop the apricots in a food processor. In a medium bowl, combine the apricots and coconut. Mix well. Stir in the sweetened condensed milk. If you feel like a touch of chocolate, add the chopped chocolate and blend.

2. Using the palms of your hands, roll small amounts of the mixture into $1^{1}/_{4}$-inch balls.

3. Roll the balls in powdered sugar or cocoa. Place on a wax paper-lined jelly-roll pan. Serve immediately. Or cover with foil and refrigerate.

MAKES 24 PIECES

CHOCOLATE MINTS

When you want to offer a subtle after-dinner mint, try these. Guests will be astonished you made your own.

1½ cups semisweet chocolate chips (9 ounces)
   1 package (10 ounces) mint semisweet chocolate chips
   1 can (14 ounces) sweetened condensed milk
   1 teaspoon vanilla extract

1. In a large glass bowl, combine the semisweet chocolate chips, mint chocolate chips and sweetened condensed milk. Microwave on High for 1 minute; stir well. Microwave for 30 to 45 seconds longer, or until the chocolate is melted and the mixture is smooth when stirred. Stir in the vanilla.

2. Turn the chocolate into a foil-lined or buttered 8-inch square baking pan. Refrigerate until firm, 30 to 60 minutes. When set, cut into 25 squares. Store, tightly covered, in the refrigerator.

MAKES 25 CHOCOLATE MINTS

CHOCOLATE RASPBERRY BON BONS

These sweets are a favorite at our house. You can mix and shape them in minutes. They're perfect when you want just a little bite for dessert. Keep these in mind also to wrap up on a moment's notice for a hostess or other gift.

1 package (9 ounces) chocolate wafer cookies
$\frac{1}{2}$ cup sweet ground chocolate and cocoa mix (such as Ghirardelli) or sweetened cocoa mix
$\frac{1}{3}$ cup Chambord or other raspberry-flavored liqueur
2 tablespoons light corn syrup
$1\frac{1}{2}$ cups finely chopped pecans or walnuts

1. In a food processor, grind the cookies to fine crumbs. Add the chocolate, Chambord and corn syrup and process until the mixture sticks together. Transfer to a medium bowl.

2. Add 1 cup of the nuts and stir until well mixed. With your hands, roll into $1\frac{1}{4}$-inch balls.

3. Roll the balls in the remaining chopped nuts. Place on a wax paper-lined jelly-roll pan. Serve immediately or refrigerate until serving time. Store, covered, in the refrigerator.

MAKES ABOUT 3 DOZEN BON BONS

PEANUT BUTTER BALLS

These are yummy—bet you can't eat just one!

1 cup chunky peanut butter
1 cup plus 2 to 3 tablespoons powdered sugar
3 tablespoons heavy cream
$1/2$ cup miniature semisweet chocolate chips

1. Place the peanut butter in a medium glass bowl. Microwave on High for 30 to 40 seconds to soften.

2. Stir in 1 cup of the powdered sugar and the cream until well blended. Add the chocolate chips and stir until well mixed.

3. Roll the peanut butter cream into 1-inch balls. Place on a wax paper-lined baking sheet. Sift the remaining powdered sugar over the balls or roll them in sifted powdered sugar. Store, covered, in the refrigerator.

MAKES 28 PEANUT BUTTER BALLS

QUICK ROCKY ROAD CANDY

Although this goes together in minutes with a little help from the microwave oven, you'll need to refrigerate it for at least an hour before serving. This is a good recipe to let children make.

1 package (12 ounces) semisweet chocolate chips
1 can (14 ounces) sweetened condensed milk
2 squares (1 ounce each) unsweetened chocolate
3 cups miniature marshmallows
1 cup chopped walnuts or pecans

1. In a 2-quart glass bowl, combine the chocolate chips and sweetened condensed milk. Break up the unsweetened chocolate and add to the bowl. Microwave on High for 1 minute; stir well. Microwave for $\frac{1}{2}$ to 1 minute longer, or until the chocolate is melted and the mixture is smooth when stirred.

2. Mix in the marshmallows and nuts. Spread evenly in a 9-inch square or an 11-by-7-inch baking pan.

3. Refrigerate 1 hour or longer, until firm. Cut into squares or rectangles.

MAKES 4 DOZEN OR MORE PIECES OF CANDY

PEANUT BUTTER FUDGE

A quick candy for peanut butter fans. Since it's made completely in the microwave, it's a good recipe to teach young children to make themselves.

1 package (11.5 ounces) milk chocolate chips
1 cup chunky peanut butter
1 can (14 ounces) sweetened condensed milk
1 teaspoon vanilla extract

1. In a medium glass bowl, combine the chocolate chips, peanut butter and sweetened condensed milk. Microwave on High for 1 minute. Stir well. Microwave on High for 35 to 45 seconds longer, or until the mixture is melted and smooth when stirred.

2. Stir in the vanilla until blended. Scrape the fudge into a foil-lined 8-inch square pan.

3. Refrigerate until set, 30 to 60 minutes. Cut into 25 squares. Keep any leftovers refrigerated.

MAKES 25 PIECES OF FUDGE

PRETZEL PEANUT CHOCOLATE CANDIES

These bon bons are quick to assemble, but you'll need to refrigerate them a short time before eating so the chocolate sets up. Make them before dinner, and they'll be ready in time for dessert.

1 package (12 ounces) semisweet chocolate chips
1/3 cup smooth or chunky peanut butter
1 1/2 cups broken pieces (1/2 inch) thin stick pretzels
3/4 cup unsalted dry roasted peanuts

1. In a medium glass bowl, combine the chocolate chips and peanut butter. Microwave on High for 1 1/2 to 2 minutes, or until the chocolate is melted and smooth when stirred.

2. Stir in the pretzel pieces and peanuts, mixing to coat completely. Drop by heaping teaspoonfuls 1 inch apart onto 2 wax paper-lined jelly-roll pans.

3. Refrigerate for about 30 to 45 minutes, or until the chocolate is set before serving.

MAKES 24 CANDIES

Chocolate Coconut Macadamia Drops

These candies couldn't be faster to make, but allow 10 to 15 minutes in the fridge for them to set up before serving. They are great to pass with a bowl of fresh raspberries, strawberries or assorted fruits or with ice cream or sorbet. They are also ideal for a festive party dessert tray.

6 ounces bittersweet chocolate, cut up
4 ounces white chocolate, cut up
1 jar (7 ounces) macadamia nuts, coarsely chopped
1 cup shredded coconut

1. In a 1½-quart glass bowl, combine the bittersweet and white chocolates. Microwave on High for 2 to 3 minutes, stirring twice, until the chocolates are melted and smooth when stirred.

2. Stir in the nuts and coconut, mixing well. Drop the mixture by heaping teaspoonfuls onto wax paper-lined baking sheets.

3. Refrigerate 10 to 15 minutes, or until the candies are firm.

Makes 30 candies

PEACHY DESSERT DRINK

Enjoy this cool, creamy beverage in summer and winter, using fresh or canned fruit, as appropriate for the season. Garnish with a peach slice, maraschino cherry and whipped cream.

2 ripe fresh peaches or 1 cup drained canned sliced peaches
1 tablespoon sugar (when using fresh peaches)
2 cups crushed ice
3 generous scoops vanilla or butter pecan ice cream (about
   1½ cups)
2 tablespoons light rum or peach liqueur

1. Peel the fresh peaches by submerging them in boiling water for 30 seconds, or until the skin puckers. Rinse with cold water and slip off the skins. Cut the peaches into slices, discarding the pits.

2. In a blender container or food processor, combine the peach slices, sugar, crushed ice, ice cream and rum. Process until well blended and as smooth as possible. Divide between 2 stemmed glasses and serve immediately.

2 SERVINGS

CHOCOCOFFEE PICK-ME-UP

When you want a quick coffee drink instead of dessert, try this delicious chocolate rendition.

1/4 cup semisweet chocolate chips
2 tablespoons heavy cream
2 cups freshly brewed hot coffee
Sweetened whipped cream (from a pressurized can)
Ground nutmeg or cinnamon

1. In a 4-cup glass measure, combine the chocolate and 2 tablespoons cream. Microwave on High for 40 to 50 seconds, or until melted and smooth when stirred.

2. Whisk in the hot coffee until well blended. Pour into 2 coffee cups or mugs.

3. Top each with a big dollop of the whipped cream and dust with the nutmeg.

2 SERVINGS

BANANA YOGURT SHAKE

My teenage son liked this dessert shake and didn't guess it contained yogurt. He kept asking for more!

1 banana
1 container (8 ounces) raspberry yogurt
1 cup ice cubes
1 teaspoon vanilla extract
  Sweetened whipped cream (from a pressurized can)

1. Peel the banana and cup it into chunks.

2. Place the banana into a blender container along with the yogurt, ice cubes and vanilla. Blend on high until smooth, stopping once and scraping down the sides.

3. Serve in a tall glass, topped with a dollop of whipped cream.

2 SERVINGS

ICED MOCHA

This is a homemade facsimile of the iced mocha drink that's so popular at some Los Angeles coffee shops. It's a great warm-weather dessert offering or afternoon treat. This is one drink that will not wait. Once you've finished making it, serve and consume it immediately.

> ½ cup nonfat milk
> 1 heaping rounded teaspoon instant coffee powder
> 2 tablespoons sweet ground chocolate and cocoa mix (such as Ghirardelli) or sweetened cocoa mix
> 1½ cups ice cubes or crushed ice
> Sweetened whipped cream (from a pressurized can)

1. In a small bowl, whisk together the milk, coffee powder and chocolate powder until well blended.

2. In a food processor, combine the ice cubes and milk mixture. Process until the drink is slushy and there are no longer any big chunks of ice.

3. Pour into a tall glass. Top with sweetened whipped cream and serve.

1 SERVING

NOTE: A blender can also be used; however, the food processor seems to do a better job of crushing the ice.

HOT DESSERT COFFEE

This yummy hot dessert drink warms the soul on a cold night. Tip:
If your brewed coffee does not have intense flavor, stir in
$\frac{1}{2}$ teaspoon instant coffee powder.

$\frac{3}{4}$ cup strong freshly brewed coffee
$\frac{1}{4}$ cup milk
  2 tablespoons sweet ground chocolate and cocoa mix (such
    as Ghirardelli) or sweetened cocoa mix
    Sweetened whipped cream (from a pressurized can)

1. In a 2-cup glass measure, combine the coffee, milk and
chocolate, mixing until well blended.

2. Microwave on High for $1\frac{1}{2}$ to 2 minutes, or until very hot.

3. Turn into a large coffee mug and top with a small mound of
whipped cream.

1 SERVING

BRANDIED HOT MOCHA

This dessert drink is reminiscent of Kafe-La-Te, a beverage I used to enjoy years ago at the long-gone Señor Pico restaurant in San Francisco's Ghirardelli Square.

1 cup freshly brewed hot coffee
3 tablespoons sweet ground chocolate and cocoa mix (such as Ghirardelli) or sweetened cocoa mix
2 tablespoons brandy
  Sweetened whipped cream (from a pressurized can)

1. In a large mug or cup, mix the coffee and chocolate until well blended. Microwave on High for 30 to 60 seconds or longer, if necessary, so mixture is very hot.

2. Stir in the brandy and top with a generous spritz of the whipped cream. Serve immediately.

1 SERVING

CHOCOLATE MILKSHAKE

Designed for chocophiles, this is reminiscent of a good old-fashioned shake. And it's so easy, kids can make it themselves.

1 cup chocolate ice cream (about 2 scoops)
1/3 to 1/2 cup cold low-fat chocolate milk
Sweetened whipped cream (from a pressurized can)

1. In a blender container, combine the ice cream and chocolate milk. Blend until creamy and thick, 30 to 60 seconds. Use the lesser amount of milk if you want a thicker shake.

2. To serve, squirt about 2 tablespoons whipped cream into the bottom of a tall glass. Top with the shake. Squirt more whipped cream on top. Serve immediately.

1 SERVING

PEANUT-CHOCOLATE MILKSHAKE: Prepare shake as directed above, adding 1 tablespoon chunky or creamy peanut butter to the ice cream mixture in step 1 before blending.

CHOCOLATE
GRAND MARNIER SAUCE

This sauce is versatile. Drizzle it over ice cream, fresh fruits or sorbets.

1 cup semisweet chocolate chips (6 ounces)
3 tablespoons heavy cream
3 tablespoons Grand Marnier or other orange-flavored
  liqueur

1. In a 2-cup glass measure, combine the chocolate chips, cream and Grand Marnier. Microwave on High for 1 to 1½ minutes, or until the chocolate is melted and the mixture is smooth when stirred.

2. Use immediately to top ice cream, yogurt, sorbet, fresh fruits or cake slices.

MAKES ¾ CUP SAUCE

CHOCOLATE PEANUT BUTTER SAUCE

Serve this warm over ice cream or on top of pound cake slices.

    1 package (12 ounces) semisweet chocolate chips
    1/3 cup chunky peanut butter
    1/2 cup milk
    1 teaspoon vanilla extract

1. In a medium microwave-safe glass bowl, combine the chocolate chips, peanut butter and milk. Microwave on High for 1 to 1½ minutes, stirring once, until the chocolate is melted and the mixture is thoroughly blended.

2. Stir in the vanilla. Serve immediately over ice cream, cake or cake and ice cream. Store in the refrigerator; reheat in the microwave oven before serving.

MAKES 1 3/4 CUPS SAUCE

BLUEBERRY SAUCE SUPREME

Cinnamon and blueberries are a wonderful combination. Serve this topping over ice cream, assorted fruits or dessert waffles.

2 cups fresh or frozen blueberries, rinsed and drained
2 teaspoons lemon juice, or more to taste
$1/2$ cup sugar
$3/4$ teaspoon ground cinnamon

1. In a medium nonreactive saucepan, combine the blueberries, lemon juice, sugar, cinnamon and $1/4$ cup water.

2. Cook over medium heat, stirring until the mixture boils, about 5 minutes. Serve warm or chilled over ice cream, fruits, dessert waffles, cake, etc.

MAKES ABOUT 1 $1/3$ CUPS SAUCE

JIFFY PINEAPPLE-ORANGE SAUCE

This refreshing sauce is wonderful for topping fresh fruits, pound cake, frozen yogurt or ice cream. Serve warm or at room temperature.

1 can (20 ounces) pineapple chunks packed in unsweetened juice
1 tablespoon cornstarch
3 tablespoons frozen orange juice concentrate

1. Drain the pineapple, reserving the juice. In a 1-quart glass bowl or measure, dissolve the cornstarch in the pineapple juice. Add the orange juice concentrate. Microwave on High for 2 minutes; stir well. Microwave for 1 minute longer, until thickened.

2. Stir in the pineapple chunks and microwave for 1 to 1½ minutes longer. Serve warm or at room temperature. Refrigerate any leftovers.

MAKES ABOUT 2½ CUPS SAUCE

PEANUT BUTTER SAUCE

If you adore peanut butter, try this sauce over ice cream or chocolate cake with ice cream.

1/2 cup chunky or smooth peanut butter
1/2 cup heavy cream
 2 tablespoons light corn syrup
3/4 teaspoon vanilla extract

1. In a medium glass bowl, combine the peanut butter, cream and corn syrup.

2. Microwave on High for 1 to 1 1/2 minutes, or until thoroughly blended and melted when stirred. Stir in the vanilla until well blended.

3. Serve warm or hot. Refrigerate any leftover sauce.

MAKES ABOUT 1 CUP SAUCE

PEACHY KEEN SAUCE

Use fresh or canned peaches to make this tasty sauce. Serve over angel food or pound cake slices, ice cream, fruit sorbets or strawberries.

1 can (16 ounces) cling peach slices, packed in light syrup
1/4 cup spiced peach spread or peach preserves
2 tablespoons orange juice

1. Drain the peaches.

2. In a small saucepan, combine the peach spread and orange juice. Heat to boiling over medium heat, stirring occasionally. Cook for 3 to 4 minutes, or until the mixture is thickened slightly.

3. Add the drained peach slices. Serve hot or chilled.

MAKES 2 CUPS SAUCE

BOYSENBERRY WHITE CHOCOLATE TOPPING

Use this jiffy sauce to top frozen yogurt, ice cream or cake and ice cream. It makes a nice gift when wrapped up in an attractive jar. Try other jam and liqueur combinations, depending on what you have on hand.

3/4 cup seedless boysenberry jam
2 tablespoons Chambord liqueur
1/4 cup chopped imported white chocolate

1. In a small bowl, mix together the jam and liqueur until smooth.

2. Stir in the white chocolate.

3. Serve immediately over frozen vanilla yogurt, ice cream or cake and ice cream.

MAKES 3/4 CUP TOPPING

INDEX